How to Use This Book

Look for these special features in this book:

SIDEBARS, **CHARTS**, **GRAPHS**, and original **MAPS** expand your understanding of what's being discussed—and also make useful sources for classroom reports.

FAQs answer common **F**requently **A**sked **Q**uestions about people, places, and things.

WOW FACTORS offer "Who knew?" facts to keep you thinking.

TRAVEL GUIDE gives you tips on exploring the state—either in person or right from your chair!

PROJECT ROOM provides fun ideas for school assignments and incredible research projects. Plus, there's a guide to primary sources—what they are and how to cite them.

Please note: All statistics are as up-to-date as possible at the time of publication. Population data is taken from the 2010 census.

Consultants: William Loren Katz; Doug Sackman, Professor of History, University of Puget Sound; Michael J. Valentine, Professor of Geology and Department Chair, University of Puget Sound; Robert McCoy, Associate Professor of History, Washington State University

Book production by The Design Lab

Library of Congress Cataloging-in-Publication Data
Stein, R. Conrad.
 Washington / R. Conrad Stein. — Revised edition.
    pages cm. — (America the beautiful, third series)
  Includes bibliographical references and index.
  Audience: Ages 9–12.
  ISBN 978-0-531-28297-7 (library binding : alk. paper)
  1. Washington (State)—Juvenile literature. I. Title.
  F891.3.S745 2014
  979.7—dc23   2013046229

1 2 3 4 5 6 7 8 9 10 R 24 23 22 21 20 19 18 17 16 15

Revised Edition

AMERICA ★ THE ★ BEAUTIFUL

Washington

BY R. CONRAD STEIN

Third Series, Revised Edition

Children's Press®
An Imprint of Scholastic Inc.
New York ★ Toronto ★ London ★ Auckland ★ Sydney
Mexico City ★ New Delhi ★ Hong Kong
Danbury, Connecticut

CONTENTS

THE SEAL OF THE STATE OF WASHINGTON 1889

CANADA

N
W E
S

Strait of Georgia

Strait of Juan de Fuca

Olympic Mountains

BELLINGHAM

Space Needle

Cascade Mountains

Okanogan

Columbia

Northwest Museum
of Arts & Culture

SPOKANE

Olympic
National Park

SEATTLE

WASHINGTON

Columbia
Plateau

Puget Sound

OLYMPIA

TACOMA

Mount Rainier
National Park

Yakima Electric
Railway Museum

ABERDEEN

Washington
State
Capitol

YAKIMA

Snake

Sacajawea
State Park

Grays Harbor
National Wildlife
Refuge

Yakima

Snake

WALLA WALLA

PACIFIC
OCEAN

Cowlitz

Yakima Valley

Fort Walla Walla
Museum

Lewis and Clark
Interpretive
Center

Columbia

VANCOUVER

Lewis County
Historical Museum

Mount St. Helens
Visitor Center

OREGON

QUICK FACTS

State capital: Olympia
Largest city: Seattle
Total area: 71,298 square miles
(184,661 sq km)
Highest point: Mount Rainier,
14,410 feet (4,392 m)
Lowest point: Sea level along
the Pacific Ocean

0   50
Miles

Welcome to Washington!

HOW DID WASHINGTON GET ITS NAME?

WASHINGTON

In the mid-1800s, the area that is now Washington was part of a huge region called the Oregon Territory. Authorities in Washington, D.C., decided to split Oregon into smaller territories, to make governing the area easier. They named the region Washington Territory in honor of George Washington, the first president of the United States. Of course, the nation already had the city of Washington (D.C.), which serves as its capital. A city and a state with the same name can be confusing. To this day, writers often refer to the state as Washington State to avoid mix-ups. The few settlers living in the territory at the time accepted the name "Washington" without complaint. After all, Washington is the only U.S. state named after a president.

READ ABOUT

A view of Diablo Lake
in North Cascades
National Park

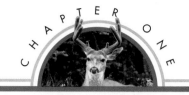

CHAPTER ONE

LAND

★

WASHINGTON HAS TOWERING MOUNTAINS, LUSH FORESTS, RUSHING RIVERS, GLISTENING LAKES, AND A LOVELY SEACOAST. The state spreads out over 71,298 square miles (184,661 square kilometers). Its landforms are wonderfully diverse, ranging from its high point—Mount Rainier—at 14,410 feet (4,392 meters) in elevation, to sea level along its long coastline. The breathtaking richness of Washington's scenery draws millions of tourists each year who delight in the state's parks and wilderness areas.

Roche Harbor at San Juan Island, part of the greater Puget Sound area

FAQ ★ ★ ★

Q: WHAT'S A SOUND?

A: The word *sound* has more that one meaning. In geography, a sound is a long, relatively wide body of water that is deep enough for ship travel.

THE GEOLOGICAL PAST

The state of Washington is bordered by Canada to the north, Idaho to the east, Oregon to the south, and the Pacific Ocean to the west. The Columbia River, one of the longest in the United States, makes up much of Washington's boundary with Oregon. Washington is roughly rectangular in shape, with a big "bite" taken out of its northwest corner. This bite is Puget Sound, a huge bay in the Pacific that is filled with islands and rocky outcrops.

Washington is part of a region called the Pacific Northwest. The region lies in the northwest corner of the United States and includes Washington, Oregon, Idaho, and western Montana.

Washington Geo-Facts

Along with the state's geographical highlights, this chart ranks
Washington's land, water, and total area compared to all other states.

Total area; rank . . . . . 71,298 square miles (184,661 sq km); 18th
Land area; rank . . . . . 66,449 square miles (172,102 sq km); 20th
Water area; rank . . . . . . 4,849 square miles (12,559 sq km); 11th
Inland water; rank . . . . . . 1,646 square miles (4,263 sq km); 14th
Coastal water; rank . . . . . 2,537 square miles (6,571 sq km); 2nd
Territorial water; rank . . . . 666 square miles (1,725 sq km); 12th
Geographic center . . . . Chelan County, 10 miles (16 km)
west-southwest of Wenatchee
Latitude . . . . 45°32' N to 49° N
Longitude . . . . 116°57' W to 124°48' W
Highest point . . . . Mount Rainier, 14,410 feet (4,392 m),
located in Pierce County
Lowest point . . . . .Sea level along the Pacific Ocean
Largest city . . . . .Seattle
Longest river . . . . .Columbia River

Source: U.S. Census Bureau, 2010 census

**Rhode Island, the smallest state,
could fit inside Washington 46 times.**

Millions of years ago, the Pacific Northwest came into
being as fiery volcanoes rose out of the sea. In a period of
geological violence, landmasses collided to form mountain ranges we now call the Cascades and the Rockies.
Finally, the land calmed. The soil sprouted trees and
grasses, and eventually animals roamed the land.

Most of the Pacific Northwest was carved slowly and
steadily over millions of years, as wind, water, and glaciers eroded the land. But one huge area in present-day
Washington was created much more quickly. If you go
200 miles (322 km) east of Seattle, you'll see mostly flat

GEOLOGIST ON A MISSION

J Harlen Bretz (1882–1981) was a geologist who was born in Michigan and moved to Seattle, where he taught high school science. Bretz enjoyed hiking, especially in the Channeled Scablands region. The odd formations there sparked his scientific curiosity. He was convinced that the canyons, boulders, and huge potholes could not have been formed by the forces of gradual **erosion**. In the 1920s, he produced the theory that the Scablands were created eons ago by a powerful flood—a megaflood—one of the greatest in Earth's long history. At first, other geologists dismissed Bretz's ideas, but today, he is hailed as the first geologist to have uncovered the secrets of the Scablands.

farmland. Then, near Coulee City, the scenery changes with dramatic suddenness. Deep canyons gouge the earth. Granite boulders weighing more than 100 tons lie scattered about. Potholes—formations that look like giant circular swimming pools, appear on otherwise unbroken ground. This rugged area in eastern Washington is called the Channeled Scablands.

For years, the land puzzled **geologists**. What forces in the earth could have formed the Scablands?

Channeled Scablands in Lyons Ferry Park

WORDS TO KNOW

erosion *the wearing away of rock or soil by wind, water, or other factors*

geologists *scientists who study the history of Earth*

A pond below Dry Falls near Coulee City

Most geologists now believe that the area was formed by a series of giant floods.

To the east, in present-day Montana, there once stood a huge lake that held as much water as Lake Erie and Lake Ontario combined. The lake was locked in place by mountains and a wall of ice more than one-half mile (0.8 km) high. As temperatures warmed, the wall of ice broke or floated free and triggered a monumental flood. The lake became a great moving mountain of water. It raced toward the Pacific Ocean, scraping out the canyons and gorges of the Channeled Scablands along the way. As temperatures cooled, the dam of ice again grew and the giant lake reformed—only to pour out in another huge flood as temperatures again rose. This cycle of flooding occurred dozens of times between 15,000 and 13,000 years ago.

SEE IT HERE!

DRY FALLS

Near Coulee City, in the heart of the Scablands, rises a cliff called Dry Falls. It was once a waterfall. At the end of the last ice age, when this waterfall was active, it was the most powerful waterfall on Earth. Dry Falls is as high as a 40-story building and more than five times wider than the majestic Niagara Falls of New York. Today, visitors stand at the base of the cliff and imagine what this spectacular waterfall looked and sounded like thousands of years ago.

Deer graze in Olympic National Park.

WORDS TO KNOW

plateau *an elevated part of the earth with steep slopes*

strait *a narrow passageway of water that connects larger bodies of water*

LAND REGIONS

Geologists divide Washington into six distinct regions: the Olympic Mountains, the Coast Range, the Puget Sound Lowlands, the Cascade Mountains, the Columbia **Plateau**, and the Rocky Mountains.

The Olympic Mountains

The Olympic Mountains region in the northwest part of the state is rugged and wildly beautiful. The **Strait** of Juan de Fuca, a finger-shaped body of water in Puget Sound,

Washington Topography

Use the color-coded elevation chart to see on the map Washington's high points (dark red to orange) and low points (green to dark green). Elevation is measured as the distance above or below sea level.

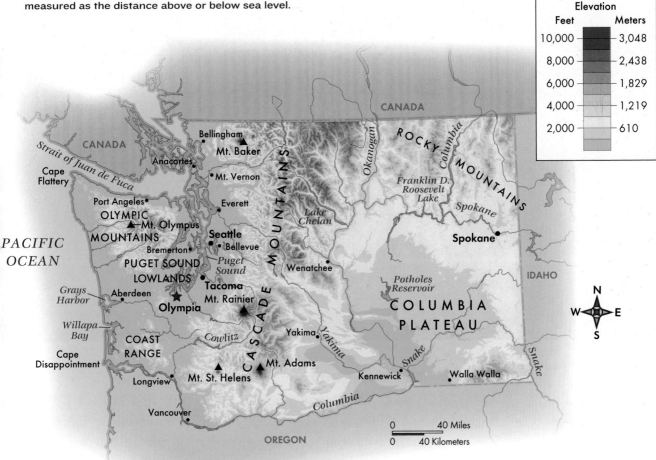

Elevation	
Feet	Meters
10,000	3,048
8,000	2,438
6,000	1,829
4,000	1,219
2,000	610

forms its northern border, and the Pacific Ocean splashes on its west. The vast Olympic National Park sprawls over much of this region. Here is some of the most untamed and untouched land found anywhere in the United States. Mount Olympus rises in the region's center.

At 7,965 feet (2,428 m) above sea level, Mount Olympus would be a large mountain in most states, but in mountainous Washington, Olympus is puny. Washington's Mount Rainier stands almost twice as high.

Tulips growing in the fertile soil of Skagit County

Puget Sound is home to roughly 210 species of fish and 100 species of seabirds.

HIKING THE COAST

Washington's Pacific coastline, from Oregon to Canada, is 157 miles (253 km) long. Jet planes zip over this coast in minutes. But a hiker faces a far different challenge. Because of Washington's many inlets, peninsulas, and islands, the state has more than 3,000 miles (4,828 km) of total shoreline.

The Coast Range

The Coast Range rises in the southwest corner of the state. Because the Coast Range is forested, it has long been valuable for its timber. The forested Willapa Hills and peaceful Willapa Bay are highlights of this region.

The Puget Sound Lowlands

The Puget Sound Lowlands is a low region that is sandwiched between the Olympic Mountains and the Cascade Mountains. True to its name, the lowlands are mostly flat, in stark contrast to the nearby mountainous landscape. The cities of Seattle, Tacoma, and Olympia are all in the Puget Sound Lowlands.

The Cascade Mountains

The Cascade Mountain range cuts across Washington from north to south, serving as the state's spine. Washington's highest mountains—Rainier, Adams, Baker, Glacier Peak, and St. Helens—all stand in the Cascades. These towering peaks are covered with snow all year long. On clear days, the snowy top of Mount Rainier can be seen from Seattle, which is almost 60 miles (97 km) away.

The Columbia Plateau

The Columbia Plateau, Washington's largest land region, passes through the southeastern part of the state. Below the surface are hardened beds of lava that oozed from the earth thousands of years ago. This field of lava rock is among the largest found anywhere on Earth. Above the layer of lava is some of the state's richest topsoil. Farmers on the Columbia Plateau grow fruits and grains and raise cattle and dairy cows. The Blue Mountains, which are low-lying by Washington standards, rise in the south near the border with Oregon.

The Rocky Mountains

The Rocky Mountains, a large mountain chain that runs from Canada to New Mexico, cuts across northeastern Washington State. In Washington, the Rockies are also called the Columbia Mountains because the Columbia River runs through the heart of the mountains. Many important minerals have been mined from the Columbia Mountains, including gold, silver, copper, and lead. The Colville National Forest, a dense woodland that embraces more than 50 lakes, is a highlight of Washington's Rocky Mountain region.

There is more snow and ice on Mount Rainier than on all the other Cascade Mountains put together.

CLIMATE

When outsiders picture Washington, they may imagine a wet state where rain, or at least drizzle, is almost constant. This image is only partially true. The Cascade Mountains divide the state into two weather zones. Air coming inland from the Pacific Ocean is moist. When that air meets the Cascades, it rises and loses its moisture in the form of rain and snow. Because of this, the land on the western side of the Cascades tends to be wet, whereas the land east of the mountains is dry and even desertlike in some areas.

Mountain ranges also affect temperatures. Winds coming off the Pacific are generally warm. The air gets much colder as it climbs the Cascades and blows eastward. This produces a large temperature difference in cities on opposite sides of the mountains. Seattle, west of the Cascades, has an average temperature in January of

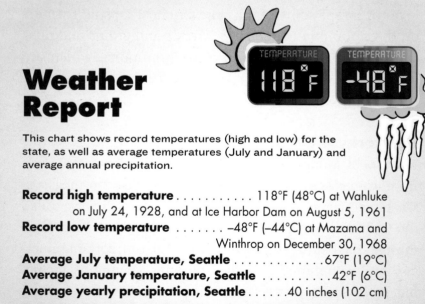

Weather Report

This chart shows record temperatures (high and low) for the state, as well as average temperatures (July and January) and average annual precipitation.

Record high temperature . . . . 118°F (48°C) at Wahluke on July 24, 1928, and at Ice Harbor Dam on August 5, 1961
Record low temperature . . . . –48°F (–44°C) at Mazama and Winthrop on December 30, 1968
Average July temperature, Seattle . . . . .67°F (19°C)
Average January temperature, Seattle . . . . .42°F (6°C)
Average yearly precipitation, Seattle . . . . . .40 inches (102 cm)

Source: National Climatic Data Center, NESDIS, NOAA, U.S. Department of Commerce

A skier in the deep snow of Crystal Mountain

about 42 degrees Fahrenheit (6 degrees Celsius). Spokane, east of the mountains, has a chilly average January temperature of 30°F (–1°C).

Roughly one-third of Washington's land area lies west of the Cascades, and that area is moist and mild in the winter and moderate in the summer. About two-thirds of the state spreads out east of the mountains and is drier and colder in the winter and hot in the summer.

During the winter months, an occasional snowstorm will hit Seattle and other cities west of the Cascades. Freezing rain and snow are common in Spokane, Pullman, and other cities in eastern Washington. Huge quantities of snow accumulate on the Cascade Mountains themselves, delighting skiers.

In the winter of 1998–1999, 95 feet (29 m) of snow fell on Mount Baker in northern Washington. That's the most snowfall ever measured in a single season in the United States.

Washington National Park Areas

This map shows some of Washington's parks, monuments, preserves, and other areas protected by the National Park Service.

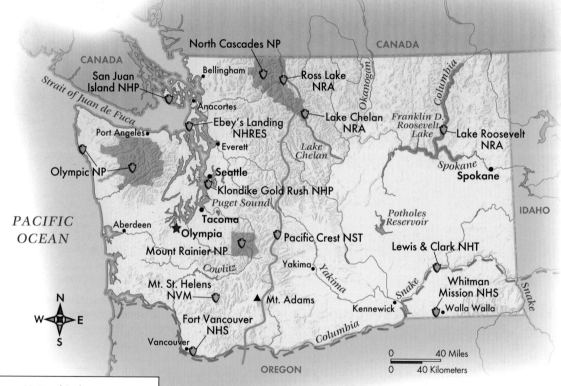

National Park area	
NHP	National Historical Park
NHRES	National Historical Reserve
NHS	National Historic Site
NHT	National Historic Trail
NP	National Park
NRA	National Recreation Area
NST	National Scenic Trail
NVM	National Volcanic Monument

PLANT LIFE

Washington's nickname is the Evergreen State. Forests—consisting mainly of firs, hemlocks, pine trees, and other evergreens—spread over more than half of Washington's land area. The densest forests are found on the western slopes of the Olympic Mountains, which receive abundant rainfall. Trees grow so close together in the Olympics

that little sun reaches the ground, even on bright days. Wildflowers such as Indian paintbrush, lupines, and goldenrod bloom on hillsides.

A black-tailed deer in Olympic National Park

ANIMAL LIFE

Wild animals abound in Washington's woodlands. Forests are home to white-tailed deer, black-tailed deer, and mule deer. Rocky Mountain and Roosevelt elk roam in the wilderness along with bighorn sheep and mountain goats. The only herd of woodland caribou outside of Alaska makes its home in Washington. Black bears are common, and even grizzly bears are sometimes seen. Beavers, badgers, and muskrats are found near the rivers. Small animals such as rabbits, squirrels, and chipmunks thrive in Washington.

A great blue heron rests on the bow of a boat near Seattle.

ENDANGERED SPECIES

Several species in Washington are in danger of becoming extinct. These include the American white pelican, spotted owl, gray wolf, grizzly bear, humpback whale, and woodland caribou. A few of these animals are making a comeback. The gray wolf had virtually disappeared from Washington by the 1930s because of trapping and hunting. But after many years of being protected, wolves have recently reappeared in the northern Cascades. Once again, visitors to the area can hear their mournful howl.

A wide variety of birds live in Washington, including pheasants, jays, tanagers, kingfishers, and grouse. Ducks and herons thrive in the state's many wetlands, while hawks and eagles soar overhead, and gulls and petrels search for food along the shore. The bright yellow feathers of the willow goldfinch, the state bird, can be seen in fields, along rivers, and in backyards.

Among the state's freshwater fish are trout, whitefish, and sturgeon. Off Washington's seacoast swim cod, flounder, porpoises, and salmon. Whales also live in the nearby ocean waters. Coastal towns such as Westport are famed whale-watching centers. Seals and sea lions frolic on the beaches and in the waters in the Puget Sound region.

Gray wolf

PROTECTING THE ENVIRONMENT

Washington, like every other state, faces challenges protecting its environment. Many environmental problems are caused by people going about everyday tasks. For example, too many cars clog the roads in the Seattle-Tacoma region, creating drifting clouds of pollution.

Logging is important to the state's economy, but it can harm forests and the animals that live there. Logging is carefully controlled. Several trees are planted for every one that is logged, and state laws protect most old-growth forests (forests of trees more than 150 years old). Although Washington's logging industry has been active for more than 100 years, large areas of old-growth wilderness still stand in the state. The Evergreen State is a beautiful place, and the people of Washington are committed to keeping it that way.

WORDS TO KNOW

ecology *the study of relationships between living things and their environment*

runoff *water from rain or snow that flows over the ground and into streams*

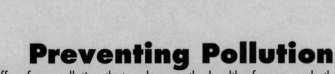

Preventing Pollution

Puget Sound suffers from pollution that endangers the health of orcas and other sea creatures. Many people have blamed this pollution on spills from oil tankers. But a 2007 study showed that oil tanker spills accounted for only 4 percent of the oil in the sound. "What that shows is we're being diligent in terms of prevention" of oil spills, says Josh Baldi of the state's Department of **Ecology**. "We should not rest on that. We need to be as diligent about other types of pollution."

Much of the rest of the oil and other pollutants in Puget Sound come from **runoff**. After rain falls, it runs across roads and parking lots, lawns and fields, picking up pollution along the way. This polluted water then runs down storm drains or into streams that flow into rivers that empty into Puget Sound.

To prevent pollutants from entering runoff, people should quickly mop up spilled oil, antifreeze, and other fluids from their cars rather than hosing them down storm drains. They should also limit the amount of chemicals they use on their lawns and in their homes. Everyone in the region is responsible for reducing the amount of pollution that enters Puget Sound.

READ ABOUT

Native American
artifacts on display
at the Moses
Lake Museum
and Art Center

c. 18,000 BCE

*The first people may have
reached North America*

▲ **c. 10,000 BCE**
*The first people arrive in
what is now Washington*

c. 8000 BCE

*Early Native people
establish a settlement
near Moses Lake*

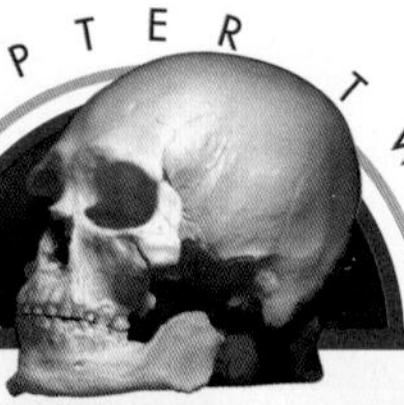

CHAPTER TWO

FIRST PEOPLE

★

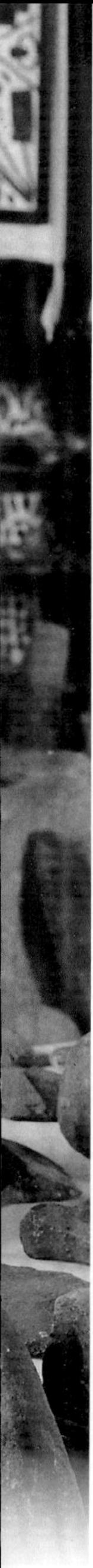

THE FIRST HUMANS PROBABLY REACHED NORTH AMERICA ABOUT 20,000 YEARS AGO. At the time, a great ice age gripped the earth. So much of the world's water was frozen that sea levels were lower. As a result, a stretch of land rose above the water's surface in the Bering Strait, between Asia and what is now Alaska. Asians likely crossed this land bridge to North America and gradually spread out over the continent.

c. 1 CE

Cultures of peoples east and west of the Cascades diverge

Early 1700s ▸

People in the Pacific Northwest acquire horses

Early 1700s

Traders bring metal tools to the region

KENNEWICK MAN

Some experts believe that humans did not arrive in North America in a single migration across the Bering Strait, but rather that they came in a series of migrations from different places. One piece of evidence they have is a set of bones discovered near Kennewick, Washington, on the northern bank of the Columbia River in 1996. The Kennewick Man skeleton is 9,000 years old. It is the oldest and most complete skeleton ever found in North America. The skull of Kennewick Man does not resemble that of modern Native Americans. It more closely resembles that of people of South Asia or the islands off the coast of Asia. Other skulls found that are at least 8,000 years old also show diversity. Does this mean that people migrated to North America from various parts of Asia? Scientists continue to search for answers.

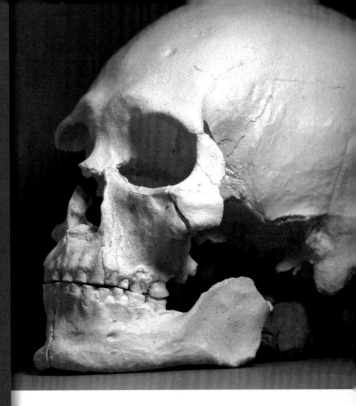

A plastic casting of the skull of Kennewick Man, found along the Columbia River in 1996

The giant beavers that once inhabited the Pacific Northwest and other parts of North America were more than 7 feet long (2 m) and weighed as much as a modern bear. They became extinct thousands of years ago.

WORD TO KNOW

archaeologists *people who study the remains of past human societies*

EARLY SETTLEMENTS

The first people probably arrived in what is now Washington about 12,000 years ago. The newcomers hunted the many animals that lived in the region. Some of the animals, including mammoths, mastodons, and giant beavers, are now extinct. These early people probably lived in bands of 20 to 50 people. They took shelter in caves or canyons.

Gradually, the first people established permanent settlements. Evidence of these settlements can be found around the state. One well-established settlement was near the town of Moses Lake in eastern Washington. At Moses Lake, **archaeologists** have found knives, hammers, and other tools made from animal bones. These objects were made some 10,000 years ago, when the knives were used to carve meat from bison that hunters had killed. Some ancient people were also excellent fishers. At a site along the Columbia River, the bones of more than 200,000 salmon have been uncovered.

CHANGING CULTURES

The Cascade Mountains divide Washington into two distinct regions. On the western side of the mountains, wet and warm conditions prevail, while the east is colder and drier. The sharp differences in these climates influenced the lives of ancient peoples, and the culture of the peoples east and west of the Cascades began to diverge more than 2,000 years ago. Groups that lived west of the Cascades included the Chinook, Clallam, Clatsop, Nisqually, Nooksack, and Puyallup peoples. Principal groups living east of the mountains included the Cayuse, Colville, Nez Perce, Okanogan, Spokane, and Yakama peoples.

These ancient petroglyphs are found in the Ginkgo Petrified Forest.

SEE IT HERE!

TSAGAGLALAL

Native Americans sometimes made petroglyphs, pictures carved into cliff walls or onto large rocks. In the Horsethief Lake section of Columbia Hills State Park, near the town of White Salmon, is a rock picture called Tsagaglalal, a Wishram word meaning "she who watches." Tradition says that Coyote, a trickster god, changed a powerful woman chief into stone. Since then, she has kept a watchful eye over her domain through her stony eyes.

The Washington State Department of Archaeology and Historic Preservation lists more than 28,000 archaeological sites in the state.

COASTAL PEOPLES

Coastal dwellers enjoyed lush forests and plentiful fish and game animals. Many experts claim the people of the Northwest Coast, who ranged from what is now southern Alaska to northern California, were materially the wealthiest of all Native Americans in the time before the arrival of the Europeans. The Northwest Coast people could easily feed themselves with the fish and other resources available in the region. This left them with much time to develop other aspects of their culture.

The Northwest Coast peoples were superb woodworkers, carving statues of gods and elaborate burial markers for their dead. Coastal people made canoes from huge logs. They burned the center of a log and then chiseled it out to create room for the rowers. Some canoes held as many as 60 people. The coastal people regularly used these large boats to venture into the ocean to hunt whales. People along the coast lived in villages in houses made from wooden posts covered with long strips of tree bark.

Native people living in tipis along the Columbia River

Wealthy families ruled each village. Wealth was measured by possessions such as canoes, blankets, and enslaved people. Most enslaved people had been captured during battles with rival groups. The wealthy sometimes threw lavish feasts called potlatches (from a word meaning "to give"). Honored guests at a potlatch were showered with gifts. After a potlatch, the host family might be impoverished but happy in the knowledge that they had so generously shared their goods with friends.

EASTERN PEOPLES

The lives of the people on the eastern side of the mountains were not as comfortable as those of the coastal dwellers. Gathering food was an almost constant activity for those in the more **arid** eastern lands. The easterners fished, picked berries, and hunted deer and bison. Groups moved frequently to follow herds of animals. Eastern people also made sturdy canoes and used them to travel the rivers of the region. Easterners looked forward to the time each year when migrating salmon filled the rivers. Fish were easily scooped up in nets during these times, and the people feasted.

Ancient Washingtonians were great traders, and men and women from opposite sides of the Cascade Range often met to swap goods. The site of The Dalles, along the Columbia River in present-day Oregon, was a traditional trading center. At trading posts, the people did more than exchange tools and artwork. They also discussed religion and entertained each other with music, dance, and storytelling.

Native Americans of the Pacific Northwest developed several common cultural traits. All believed in many gods and one Great Spirit who created the universe. Religious leaders, called shamans, were the

WORD TO KNOW

arid *dry*

For years, Native Americans from eastern Washington told of a legendary past when so many salmon filled the rivers that people could walk from one side to another without getting their feet wet.

Native American Peoples
(Before European Contact)

This map shows the general area of Native American peoples before European settlers arrived.

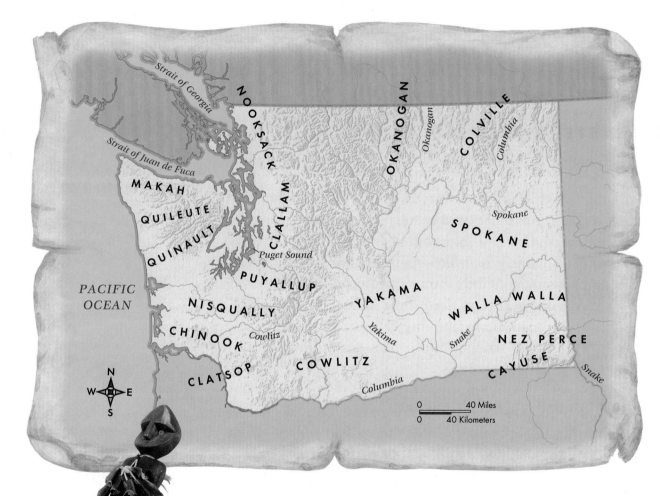

A shaman's "guardian spirit"

most important individuals in a village. Shamans could be either men or women. It was believed that shamans were born with special gifts, which allowed them to contact the dead or to converse with the many gods and spirits. Shamans also treated sick people using prayer and herbal medicines.

CHANGING TIMES

The people of the Northwest acquired horses for the first time in the early 1700s. The horses came from the Europeans who had begun settling North America. The Spanish had established New Spain (present-day Mexico) in the 1520s. Until the Spaniards arrived, there were no horses in the Americas. Some of their horses escaped or were left behind, and they eventually roamed as far north as the Pacific Northwest. Native American merchants may have also brought them. In eastern Washington, horses made hunting bison much easier.

In the early 1700s, Native American traders came from the south bearing wondrous goods—metal knives and axes much stronger than the ones used for generations in the Pacific Northwest. These, too, came from the Europeans.

At this time, Native people in the Pacific Northwest had yet to see a white person, although some occasionally saw a European ship sailing along the coast. But traders from the south told of light-skinned newcomers who were aggressive fighters and bore powerful weapons. These weapons sounded like thunder and could kill from a great distance.

Soon these newcomers would venture into what is now Washington State, where Native societies had thrived for countless generations. As the two groups came into contact, life for Native Americans would change dramatically.

Picture Yourself . . .

Seeing a Horse for the First Time

It is the late 1600s, and you live in a village in what is now western Washington. One day, a Native American trading band from the south approaches your village. The traders are leading a strange animal on a rope. The four-legged creature is bigger than a deer, but not as heavy as a bison. The animal does not try to break away from the man. Everyone from your village gathers around to look at this strange beast. Suddenly, to everyone's astonishment, one of the traders jumps on the animal's back. He rides easily while the animal gallops faster than a person can run. Where can you get one of these magnificent creatures?

READ
ABOUT

A view of Puget
Sound looking
toward the Cascade
Mountains,
early 1800s

1775

*Spanish explorer Bruno
de Heceta leads the first
group of Europeans to
set foot in what is now
Washington*

1792 ▶

*Robert Gray claims
the Washington area
for the United States*

1805

*Lewis and Clark
reach the Pacific
Ocean at the mouth
of the Columbia
River*

EXPLORATION AND SETTLEMENT

★

I N THE EARLY 1800s, MANY EUROPEAN AND U.S. EXPLORERS WERE LOOKING FOR SOMETHING. They hoped that somewhere on the continent there was a natural sea channel that would allow ships to sail from the Atlantic Ocean to the Pacific. If they could find such a route, it would provide traders with a shortcut to Asia. Explorers never found such a ship channel, but they discovered a new land— the Pacific Northwest—and hailed it as the finest land on Earth.

◄ 1836

Marcus Whitman and his wife, Narcissa (left), establish a mission church near Walla Walla

1847

Native Americans try to force whites off their land during the Cayuse War

1850

Congress passes the Donation Land Claim Act

European Exploration of Washington

The colored arrows on this map show the routes taken by explorers between 1774 and 1806.

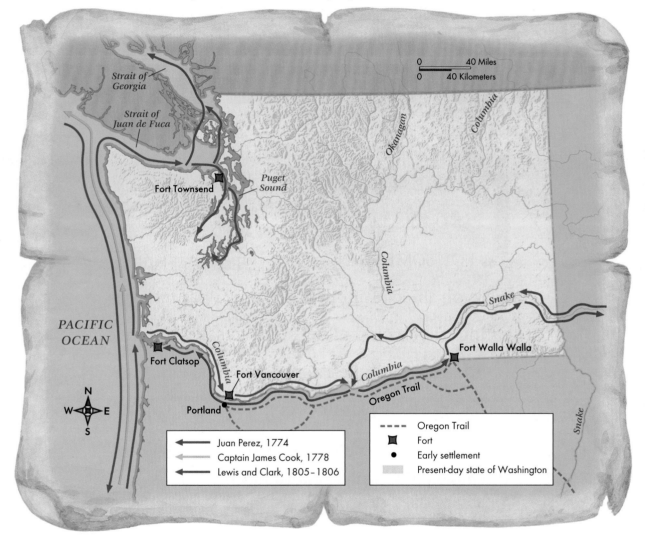

0   40 Miles
0   40 Kilometers

Strait of Georgia

Strait of Juan de Fuca

Okanagan

Columbia

Fort Townsend

Puget Sound

Columbia

PACIFIC OCEAN

Snake

Fort Walla Walla

Fort Clatsop

Columbia

Fort Vancouver

Columbia

Oregon Trail

Portland

N W E S

Snake

⬅ Juan Perez, 1774
⬅ Captain James Cook, 1778
⬅ Lewis and Clark, 1805–1806

- - - Oregon Trail
🏯 Fort
● Early settlement
▨ Present-day state of Washington

EUROPEANS ARRIVE

Crewmembers aboard a Spanish ship commanded by Juan de Fuca may have been the first Europeans to see the Pacific Northwest. De Fuca was a Greek sailing for Spain. (His birth name was Apóstolos Valerianos.) He claimed that he sailed along the Northwest coast in 1592, but he may have made up the story. Whether or not he ever reached the region, the sea passage from the Pacific Ocean to Puget Sound is called the Strait of Juan de Fuca.

In the mid-1700s, Russian fur traders established trading posts along the coast north of Washington, in what is now Alaska. Beavers and sea otters were numerous there, and the Russians traded with Native Americans for pelts. The Russian presence in the region concerned Spanish leaders, who had their own designs on the Pacific Northwest. In 1775, Bruno de Heceta led a Spanish expedition into the region. On July 14, he and some of his crew went ashore at what is now Point Grenville, becoming the first Europeans to set foot on Washington soil. The crew erected a cross on the ground and formally claimed the entire Pacific Northwest as part of the Spanish empire.

It didn't take long for Europeans to clash with Native Americans in the region. The 1775 Spanish mission began peacefully. Native Americans in canoes approached the Spanish ship, the crew greeted them, and the two peoples exchanged trinkets. But later that evening, something touched off a fight, and seven Europeans were killed in a brief battle. The Spanish ship retreated with its cannons blazing.

Great Britain, Spain's most powerful rival, also had interests in the Pacific Northwest. The British wanted to expand their fur trade into the region, and they hoped to find the Northwest Passage, which would make it easier to transport the pelts back to Europe. British explorer Captain James Cook made a sea voyage to the Pacific Northwest in 1778. Cook spotted Mount Olympus. He landed on Vancouver Island in what is now Canada but never went to Washington. In 1792, another British ship captained by George Vancouver sailed along the coast. One of Vancouver's officers, Peter Puget, entered a body

THE NORTHWEST PASSAGE

The belief in a seaway that cut through North America dated back to Christopher Columbus's first voyage in 1492. To Europeans, this great landmass stood as a hindrance to ship travel and to trade with China. Many sea voyages were launched in the 1600s and 1700s in hopes of finding a waterway to the north that they called the Northwest Passage. It was not until the 1800s that sea captains came to the conclusion that no convenient Atlantic-to-Pacific shipping lane existed in North America.

The encampment of Peter Puget, 1792

of water that was later named Puget Sound in his honor. Vancouver also gave the English names to Mount Baker, Mount Rainier, and several other Washington landmarks.

By the late 1700s, the Pacific Northwest loomed as a prize pursued by Great Britain, Russia, Spain, and France. At first, the European nations coveted the region's fur-bearing animals. European governments also dreamed of someday sending settlers to the region and establishing colonies. Meanwhile, another country—the young United States, which had only declared its independence from Great Britain in 1776—looked with interest at the Pacific Northwest as well.

AMERICAN EXPLORERS

In 1790, American sea captain Robert Gray sailed out of Boston, Massachusetts, on a ship called the *Columbia* to make the long voyage around the southern tip of South America and north toward the Pacific Northwest. Gray's journey was financed by a Boston company interested in the fur trade. The captain stopped at a bay in what is now southwestern Washington. Today, this spot is called Grays Harbor. He next took his ship into the mouth of a large river, which he named the Columbia after his ship. Gray planted the American flag along the coastline and claimed the entire region for the United States.

The *Columbia*, Robert Gray's ship, under attack by coastal Natives in the Strait of Juan de Fuca, 1792

SACAGAWEA: GUIDE THROUGH THE WILDERNESS

Explorers Lewis and Clark relied on a Shoshone woman named Sacagawea (1787?–1812), who joined the expedition when she was still a teenager. Lewis and Clark came to rely on Sacagawea (also spelled Sacajawea) to help lead them through mountain passes. She was assisted by an enslaved man named York, William Clark's companion since childhood. Sacagawea helped Lewis and Clark trade for horses with the Shoshone people. The Shoshone leader happened to be Sacagawea's brother, and she was able to introduce Lewis and Clark as her friends. Today, she is honored throughout the nation. There are more statues to her than any other woman in U.S. history.

? **Want to know more?** Visit www.factsfornow .scholastic.com and enter the keyword **Washington**.

SEE IT HERE!

LEWIS AND CLARK INTERPRETIVE CENTER

In November 1805, after an 18-month trek, the members of the Lewis and Clark expedition climbed a hill and caught their first glimpse of the Pacific Ocean. You can stand on the same hill and on a clear day see the same view from Cape Disappointment State Park, now part of the Lewis and Clark National Historical Park, near the town of Ilwaco. Nearby is the Lewis and Clark Interpretive Center, a museum that presents a slide show and displays articles dealing with the expedition.

The first school in today's Washington opened in 1832 at Fort Vancouver. It served the children of the British-owned Hudson's Bay Company.

WORD TO KNOW

latitude *the position of a place, measured in degrees north or south of the equator*

In 1804, President Thomas Jefferson sent Meriwether Lewis and William Clark on an expedition to explore the land west of the Mississippi. Lewis and Clark led a band of explorers on a trek that took them from St. Louis, Missouri, to the Pacific Ocean and back again. Most of the trip was through territory that only Native Americans had explored. The party reached the Pacific at the mouth of the Columbia River in November 1805.

COMPETING CLAIMS

Eventually Russia, Spain, and France withdrew their ownership claims on the Pacific Northwest. This left the United States and Great Britain to clash over the region, which was then called the Oregon Country.

In the 1840s, an idea called manifest destiny gripped the United States. Manifest destiny was the idea that the country was destined to expand westward to the Pacific.

California and much of the Southwest became U.S. territories after the Mexican-American War of 1846–1848. This meant that only the Oregon Country remained to be added, in order for the United States to stretch across the continent. Realistically, the British had little chance to retain their claims on Oregon. The region lay many thousands of miles from the British Isles, and American adventurers and fur traders were already streaming into the Oregon Country.

Britain was willing to negotiate. The big question became, where should the boundary between British Canada and the Oregon Country be? Some American politicians wanted to put the boundary at the **latitude** 54°40' N, which is far north, near present-day Alaska. Their slogan was "Fifty-Four Forty or Fight." In 1846, British and American diplomats were able to agree on a border at the 49th parallel, the present boundary between Washington State and Canada.

The Lewis and Clark expedition on the Columbia River, 1805

Once the United States gained the Pacific Northwest, the dreams of those who believed in manifest destiny came to pass. The nation now spread from sea to shining sea.

TRAPPERS AND MISSIONARIES

Long before Oregon Territory was officially established, American trappers ventured to the land. These so-called mountain men were hardy individuals who had been trapping animals for their fur and trading with Native Americans in the Rocky Mountain region since the 1820s.

THE PIG WAR

The 1846 treaty in which Great Britain surrendered its claims to the Pacific Northwest was vague in defining who controlled the San Juan Islands along the border with Canada. Both Great Britain and the United States claimed the island group, and both nations encouraged settlement there. Britain's Hudson's Bay Company owned a sheep farm on San Juan Island, the second-largest island in the group, but Americans were also settling there. In June 1859, a pig owned by an employee of the Hudson's Bay Company broke loose and raided the potato field of an American farmer. The enraged American farmer shot the animal. The incident caused both sides to threaten war, but British admiral Robert L. Baynes said he would not use warships "over a squabble about a pig." All-out war was averted, and the San Juan Islands are now part of Washington State.

This painting shows fur trader John McLoughlin welcoming Narcissa Whitman and Eliza Spalding to Fort Vancouver in 1836.

WORDS TO KNOW

missionaries *people who try to convert others to a religion*

immunities *natural protections against diseases*

Many **missionaries** also traveled to the region. Among the earliest missionaries were Marcus and Narcissa Whitman, who left New York and established a church near what is now Walla Walla, Washington, in 1836. Narcissa Whitman and Eliza Spalding, another missionary, were the first white women to complete the difficult overland trip to the Pacific Northwest.

Native Americans greeted the newcomers with curiosity and fear. The white Americans had interesting items to trade—iron hatchets, knives, guns, and cooking pots. But trouble soon began. The trappers and missionaries had unknowingly brought deadly diseases such as diphtheria and measles to Oregon. People in Europe and the eastern United States had long been exposed to these diseases, so they had developed **immunities** and could fight them off. They might get sick from the diseases, but they rarely died. Native Americans had never before been exposed to these diseases, and they had no such immunities. The diseases swept through Native communities, killing huge numbers of people.

The Whitmans treated both Cayuses and whites in their small clinic. Most of the white people the couple treated recovered from their illnesses, but the Indians did not. Some Cayuses came to believe that the Whitmans were deliberately killing Native Americans. On November 29, 1847, Cayuse fighters attacked the mission church. Marcus and Narcissa Whitman and 12 others were killed.

The Whitman massacre triggered the Cayuse War, which raged throughout the Oregon Country. Hundreds of pioneers banded together and attacked Cayuse villages. Five men believed to be ringleaders of the Whitman murders were captured, tried, and hanged. Sporadic wars between white settlers and Native Americans broke out in the region through the 1850s and 1860s.

THE OREGON TRAIL

Gold was discovered in California in 1848. The prospect of striking it rich drew thousands of Americans to California. The gold rush started America's westward movement to the Pacific Coast. During this time, adventurers, gold seekers, and young, mostly male, fortune hunt-

MOUNTAIN MEN

Rugged trappers and scouts known as mountain men began working in the Rocky Mountains in the early 1800s. Some became heroic figures because they seemed fearless and did not care about the everyday comforts of home. Mountain men lived alone for months among the canyons and peaks as they hunted and trapped. Prominent mountain men included Kit Carson, John Colter, and Jedediah Smith. The mountain men helped map the Rocky Mountains, and they were part of a colorful chapter in American history.

Kit Carson

A journey on the Oregon Trail was difficult and could take up to six months.

ers raced to California. Meanwhile, families and farmers in the East caught "Oregon fever" and moved west, ready to start new lives in the distant land.

Americans from the East, heading for either California or the Oregon Country, followed the Oregon Trail. They were led by guides such as Moses Harris, an African American who had been an explorer and trapper in the western mountains since the early 1820s.

The Oregon Trail began in Independence, Missouri, and wound 2,000 miles (3,219 km) through tall-grass prairies, mountains, and forests. Near Fort Hall in present-day Idaho, the trail split. California-bound travelers took the California Trail, which ran south, and those headed for Oregon trekked north. By covered wagon, the trip to the West Coast took about six months.

Travelers on the Oregon Trail faced blinding winter snowstorms and suffocating desert heat. But the biggest danger was disease, such as cholera, which spread quickly from person to person. Travelers sometimes counted the graves along the trail. Still, the settlers kept coming. They were accompanied by mooing cows, clucking chickens, and yapping dogs that raced up and down the long line of wagons. Many people arrived in the future state of Washington from Pike County, Missouri, and they sang a song that was popular along the Oregon Trail:

Oh, don't you remember sweet
*   Betsy from Pike,*
Who crossed the big mountains
*   with her lover Ike.*
With two yoke of oxen, a big yellow dog,
A tall Shanghai rooster, and one spotted hog?

GEORGE WASHINGTON BUSH: PIONEER

A prominent pioneer in early Washington was George Washington Bush (1790?–1863). A free black man, Bush traveled to the Oregon Country to escape the **prejudice** and racist laws he encountered in the eastern states. In 1845, he established a farm and a sawmill near Tumwater, Washington. He was well liked among the pioneers because he always fed and assisted weary travelers. He applied for free land under the Donation Land Claim Act but was denied a grant because he was African American. His white friends asked the territorial government to make an exception in Bush's case, and he was given land in 1855.

? **Want to know more?** Visit www.factsfornow.scholastic.com and enter the keyword **Washington**.

In 1850, Congress passed the Donation Land Claim Act, which allowed American citizens in the Oregon Country to claim as many as 640 acres (260 ha) of free land. This land grant was written in 19th-century terms that recognized only white males as citizens. Single women, African Americans, Asians, and Native Americans were not eligible for the free land. Still, people poured across the plains and the mountains, starting new lives in the West.

WORD TO KNOW

prejudice *an unreasonable hatred or fear of others based on race, religion, ethnic group, gender, or other factors*

READ ABOUT

A view of Fort
Vancouver, 1853

1852

Seattle is founded

1853
*Washington Territory
is established*

◄ **1877**

*Chief Joseph leads
the Nez Perce on a
prolonged retreat
toward Canada*

GROWTH AND CHANGE

★

I N 1852, A BAND OF SETTLERS LED BY
DAVID AND ARTHUR DENNY ARRIVED AT
PUGET SOUND. The Denny Party looked
in awe at the nearby towering mountains and
forests. After determining that the waters were
sufficiently deep to dock ships, the Denny brothers founded the village of Seattle, named after a
Native American leader.

1883

The Northern Pacific
Railway is completed,
connecting Tacoma
with Minnesota

1889 ▶

Washington
becomes the
42nd state

1897

Seattle booms after
gold is discovered
in Alaska

MINI-BIO

SEALTH: PEACEMAKER

Sealth (1786?–1866), also known as Seattle, was the leader of the Suquamish people who lived near Puget Sound. As a young man, Sealth was known to be a courageous fighter. As he grew older, the leader often preached peace. When wars between Europeans and Native Americans swirled around Seattle, Sealth urged both sides to negotiate, work out their differences, and avoid warfare.

 Want to know more? Visit www.factsfornow .scholastic.com and enter the keyword **Washington**.

GROWING CITIES

Vancouver, on the Columbia River, is Washington's oldest city. It was founded in 1825 as Fort Vancouver, a military barracks and trading post. The city of Olympia got its start in 1846 as a fishing and shipping outpost. Tacoma began in 1852 when a Swedish settler named Nicholas De Lin built a sawmill there. Port Townsend was founded as a shipping center in 1853 and quickly developed a reputation for rowdiness. Sailors drank, gambled, and fought each other at Port Townsend's waterfront.

Port Townsend on Puget Sound, 1878

Washington: From Territory to Statehood
(1848–1889)

This map shows the original Washington Territory and the area (in yellow) that became the state of Washington in 1889.

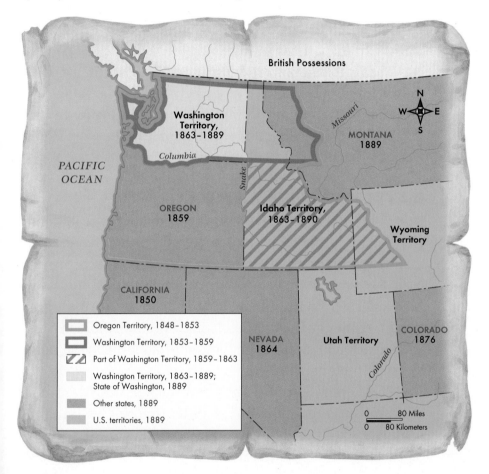

By 1853, about 4,000 white settlers lived in the region, and the U.S. Congress officially established Washington Territory. Olympia was named the capital. The territory originally included parts of what are now northern Idaho and western Montana. It was not until 1863 that the state gained the borders it has today.

The state's first public library opened in Olympia in 1853, the year Washington became a territory.

THE CIVIL WAR

After Abraham Lincoln was elected president in 1860, Southern states began withdrawing from the Union because they feared that he would outlaw slavery. They formed a new nation called the Confederate States of America. On April 12, 1861, Confederate troops attacked Fort Sumter in faraway South Carolina, and the United States exploded into the Civil War.

Washingtonians were mostly from the Northeast, and they sympathized with the Union side. Slavery, one of the issues that led to the war, had been outlawed in the Pacific Northwest since 1844. The people of the Northwest watched the bloody conflict from afar.

BATTLING FOR LAND

During the 1850s and 1860s, wars between white settlers and Native Americans frequently broke out, settled down, and then flared up again. Washington's first territorial governor, Isaac Stevens, wanted to encourage white settlement, so in 1854 and 1855, he **impelled** Washington's Native Americans to sign treaties giving up their lands. They were forced onto small reservations, although they were guaranteed the right to fish in their usual places.

This separation of whites and Native Americans did not prevent the outbreak of bitter fighting. Nisqually leader Leschi led Native people in the Puget Sound War of 1855–1856 to protest the unfair terms of the treaties. Stevens held Leschi responsible for killings that were committed during the war, even though he had not committed the crimes. As a result, he was hanged.

When gold was discovered on Native American lands in 1855, large groups of white miners flocked to the goldfields there. Native groups united under Yakama leader Kamiakin to fight off the invasion of the miners.

WORD TO KNOW

impelled *forced somebody to do something*

A Nez Perce camp outside Old Fort Walla Walla on the Columbia River

The bloody Yakima War (1855–1858) resulted in the capture and execution of many Indian leaders and a peace treaty that forced most Native Americans to move to reservations.

In the 1870s, white settlers began farming and building cabins on Nez Perce land in eastern Washington and Oregon. Nez Perce leader Chief Joseph appealed to the government to find a peaceful resolution to the land dispute, but younger Nez Perce decided to fight for their land instead and killed several settlers. The U.S. Army sent around 2,000 troops to attack the Nez Perce people. Chief Joseph led a group of 700 people, only about 200 of them fighters, on a long fighting retreat. The band bravely battled the U.S. troops as they wound 1,500 miles (2,400 km) over the Rocky Mountains. When Chief Joseph finally surrendered in October 1877, he gave a moving speech that ended, "I am tired of fighting. . . . The little children are freezing to death. . . . My heart is sick and sad. From where the sun now stands, I will fight no more forever."

Leschi, a Nisqually leader

Chief Joseph was a loyal follower of Smohalla, a Wanapum religious leader and teacher. Smohalla preached that Native Americans should reject the white people's ways, such as plowing the land or signing treaties for land. His influence spread among Native Americans in the region and lasted for years after his death in 1895.

SETTLING EASTERN WASHINGTON

The earliest pioneers in Washington Territory moved primarily to fertile, well-watered lands west of the Cascade Mountains. Settlement was slower in eastern Washington, where rain was scarce and winters harsh. Still, villages began to bloom on the plains east of the Cascade Mountains. Spokane did not have permanent settlers until 1872, when the city founder, James Nettle Glover, built a store in what is now downtown. Glover wrote, "I lived in my store building . . . [surrounded by] a beautiful prairie of bunch grass and sunflowers." In 1881, the city of Three Forks was home to just a handful of people. Three Forks changed its name to Pullman in hopes of getting financial support from the Pullman Palace Car Company in Chicago. The support never came, but Pullman grew anyway.

RAILROADS AND THE WEST

More than any other institution, railroads contributed to the growth of the American West. The first transcontinental railroad, completed in 1869, connected Sacramento, California, with the East Coast. Washingtonians watched California thrive as the railroad brought thousands of newcomers to their state. They waited eagerly for railroad companies to build a line linking their territory with the eastern United States.

Washington's railroad, the Northern Pacific Railway, was completed in 1883. The railroad linked Minnesota

Members of a Northern Pacific Railway crew, 1885

with Tacoma. The trip between those two points, which took six months by wagon, was now reduced to a mere five days. The railroad also allowed letters to reach the West much more quickly. Before the railroads, most mail to the Pacific Northwest was delivered by ships. The mail was sent down the Atlantic coast, brought across Central America, and shipped north up the Pacific coast. Letters commonly arrived in Washington Territory weeks or even months after they were written. Once the railroad connected Washington to the East, letters arrived in little more than a week.

Railroads meant money. Wherever the railroad went, prosperity was sure to follow. The people of Seattle fumed when the leaders of the Northern Pacific Railway decided to end the line at Tacoma instead of their city. Seattle residents feared the railroad's decision would leave their city to wither and die.

A TOWN ON WHEELS

Yakima was a settlement of about 500 people and 100 buildings when the newly built railroad erected a station 4 miles (6 km) north of town. So the people of Yakima put their buildings on skids and had teams of horses pull them to the railroad station. Yakima stores continued to sell goods as they rolled along to their new location. The town's hotel even rented out rooms when the buildings stopped for the night.

With the completion of the Northern Pacific, the people of Washington Territory caught "railroad fever." Spokane flourished because the train ran almost right through its center. A local newspaper boasted, "New dwellings, new stores, and new manufacturing establishments are springing up like magic."

Railroads linked cities, brought in people, and allowed farmers to ship goods around the country. By 1889, Washington Territory's population topped 350,000, an increase of 375 percent in 10 years. The territory was now ready to become a state.

A view of Spokane, which grew rapidly after the completion of the Northern Pacific Railway.

STATEHOOD

On November 11, 1889, President Benjamin Harrison proclaimed Washington the nation's 42nd state. But when Elisha P. Ferry, who was to be the new governor, arrived at the telegraph office in Olympia to receive the official announcement of statehood, he found that leaders in Washington, D.C., had sent the telegram collect. Governor Ferry complained because he had to pay 61 cents from his own pocket to pick up the telegram.

The year of statehood was also a year of spectacular fires. On June 6, 1889, a fire broke out in a glue pot owned by a Seattle carpenter and quickly consumed the house and neighboring houses. By the time the flames were brought under control, some 30 blocks of Seattle's business district were reduced to ashes. However, no one was killed. Two months later, another devastating fire broke out in Spokane. In both cases, the flames spread rapidly because buildings were constructed of wood. Brick buildings rose to replace wooden structures, and the state was spared disastrous urban fires in the future.

The people who lived in the new state of Washington were mostly of European descent, but some African Americans had joined the movement west. Horace Cayton and his wife, Susan, arrived in 1889, and several years later began the *Seattle Republican*, the state's first

ELISHA P. FERRY: A WASHINGTON FIRST

Like most of the other settlers in Washington at the time of statehood, Elisha Ferry (1825–1895) came from the East. Ferry was born in Michigan, settled in Illinois, and moved to Washington Territory in 1869. He served as territorial governor and then was elected the state's first governor, a position he held for four years. He is still considered one of the most distinguished governors in the state's history. Ferry County in eastern Washington is named in his honor.

? **Want to know more?** Visit www.factsfor now.scholastic.com and enter the keyword **Washington**.

The fire that devastated Seattle on June 6, 1889, burned out of control largely because the city's fire chief was out of town. He was in a neighboring city attending a fire prevention conference.

Workers at a salmon-canning factory on the Columbia River, late 1800s

successful African American newspaper. They supported many reforms, including giving women the right to vote.

Many Asians lived in Washington. Chinese immigration to the West Coast began with the California gold rush. After the gold rush died down, many Chinese people moved north to Oregon and Washington. They worked on farms and in laundries or labored on the railroads. Chinese workers were vital in the building of the Northern Pacific Railway line. They labored for long days in the blazing sun and drizzling rain. No one could doubt they were hardworking. Yet in Washington and elsewhere in the West, some white Americans thought Chinese immigrants were taking away jobs and therefore considered them untrustworthy.

Chinese people in Washington worked for low wages, toiling in laundries and fish-canning companies. European American workers believed that competition with Chinese workers lowered their own wages. In 1885, anti-Chinese mobs raged through Tacoma's Chinese neighborhood, burning buildings and looting stores. The city's entire Chinese American population was forced out of town. Similar riots took place a year later in Seattle. Many of Seattle's Chinese residents, who had lived there for years, were forced to flee.

For the most part, Washington's economy boomed in the late 1800s. Timber was a leading industry as people cut down the state's towering trees. Coal companies prospered largely by selling coal to the railroads and to steamships. Fishing, mining, and shipbuilding made great strides.

A new fever—"apple fever"—gripped the farms of Washington. Americans began demanding the crispy apples that were grown in Washington and then shipped around the country by railroad. Washington soon became the nation's largest apple producer.

Education expanded during this time as well. In the first year after Washington became a state, several high schools, rare in territorial times, were built. Today's Washington State University opened at Pullman in 1892. In the early 1890s, state-supported teachers colleges opened at Cheney, Ellensburg, and Bellingham.

Washington apples

In 1897, a ship docked at Seattle carrying an exciting cargo—gold! Some reports, probably exaggerated, claimed the ship carried "a ton of gold." The precious metal came from Alaska, and it triggered a new gold rush. Excited miners from around the world flocked to Seattle in order to catch ships bound for the Alaskan goldfields. The gold seekers bought supplies in Seattle's stores, and the city enjoyed a boom. In 10 years, Seattle's population doubled. The young state, and its leading city, were prospering.

READ ABOUT

Crowds gather at
the Alaska-Yukon-
Pacific Exposition
in Seattle, 1909.

GIVE WOMEN THE BALLOT
For the   Sake of
THE CHILDREN

1910 ▲
*Washington passes a
law allowing women to
vote in state elections*

1933
*Work begins on
Bonneville Dam
on the Columbia
River*

1942–45
*Japanese Americans
are forced into
internment camps
during World War II*

CHAPTER FIVE

MORE MODERN TIMES

★

I N 1909, THE ALASKA-YUKON-PACIFIC EXPOSITION OPENED IN SEATTLE. It was a great fair that showcased Washington's amazing progress in just 20 years of statehood. More than 3 million people from around the world attended the exposition. Visitors saw a beautiful state filled with energetic people. The official theme of the fair represented the attitude of hardworking, plain-speaking Washingtonians: "The truth is good enough."

1962 ►

The Seattle World's Fair opens

1974

A court decision guarantees Native Americans the right to fish in traditional areas

2013

Leaks are found in tanks of radioactive waste at the Hanford nuclear site

Workers using steam locomotives and other engines to haul logs from the forests of Washington

PROGRESS AND PROBLEMS

In the early 20th century, eastern Washington and western Washington continued to develop as if they were separate states. The forests of western Washington provided lumber. Shipping in Puget Sound expanded as the state's population and industry grew. Fishing and fish processing were also important in the western part of the state. Farming was the major enterprise in eastern Washington, but the region was hampered by a lack of rain. Irrigation came to the rescue. With the help of the federal government, dams were built in the Yakima and Okanogan valleys. Water from these irrigation projects allowed wheat to become a major crop in eastern Washington. Cities such as Pasco, Ellensburg, Yakima, Walla Walla, and Wenatchee grew as farming expanded.

As the economy developed, bankers, businesspeople, and owners of large farms thrived. Some made fortunes. Workers did not fare as well. Lumberjacks in the timber camps earned two dollars a day. Factory workers and field hands on farms were also poorly paid. The railroads, which brought prosperity to the state, hampered small farmers by charging high rates to ship their crops to city markets.

Some Washingtonians who wanted to fix these imbalances turned to the Progressive Movement. Progressive political parties were also active in many other states in the early 1900s. Progressives wanted average people to have more say in their government. Washington's progressives passed a law that created a direct primary election in which voters would choose the candidates rather than having candidates chosen by party leaders. Washington's progressives also wanted citizens to get rid of old laws, create new laws, and remove officials by a direct vote rather than having to appeal to the state legislature. Progressives also supported woman **suffrage**. By 1912, most of the ideas promoted by the Progressive Movement had become state laws.

MINI-BIO

MAY HUTTON: SUFFRAGE LEADER

May Hutton (1860–1915) was born in Ohio and made her way west in 1883, settling first in Idaho. There she ran a restaurant catering to a rough crowd of miners. A big woman, she took no nonsense from the miners, and they respected her. In 1887, she married a railroad engineer. The couple took a gamble when they bought a small share in an Idaho mine, which they worked side by side. They struck it rich, finding a small fortune in silver, lead, and zinc. In 1906, they moved to Spokane where May Hutton became involved in politics. With tireless energy, she campaigned for woman suffrage. In 1910, Washington passed a law allowing women to vote in state elections.

❓ **Want to know more?** Visit www.factsfor now.scholastic.com and enter the keyword **Washington**.

WORD TO KNOW

suffrage *the right to vote*

World War I soldiers with Seattle members of the War Camp Community Service organization, which raised money for the troops

BOOMS AND BUSTS

In 1914, World War I began in Europe. European leaders believed the war would be short, but the fighting dragged on. The United States managed to stay out of the war in its early years, but in 1917 the nation joined Great Britain, France, and other countries in fighting Germany and its allies.

That same year, Fort Lewis opened in Washington State. During World War I, some 60,000 soldiers trained at the site. The war also boosted Washington's economy by increasing the demand for goods, and wheat and lumber prices rose dramatically. In Seattle, a tiny aircraft company called Boeing grew during the war years.

When the war ended in 1918, farm prices and timber prices dropped. The demand for factory goods decreased, and thousands of workers lost their jobs. Many Washington workers turned to labor unions for help and security, and a series of labor conflicts shook the state.

The most aggressive union was the Industrial Workers of the World (IWW), also known as the Wobblies. The IWW recruited men and women of all backgrounds, including African Americans, Asians, and immigrants, into what it called One Big Union. The IWW wanted workers to control the factories. Union leaders supported powerful and sometimes violent labor strikes to force the bosses to meet workers' demands.

In February 1919, the shipyard workers of Seattle went on strike hoping to gain better pay and working conditions. The IWW then called on all working people to walk off their jobs in sympathy with the shipyard laborers. A strange hush greeted Seattle as streetcar conductors, truck drivers, factory employees, and mail carriers refused to work. The action, sometimes called the Seattle Revolution, was the first successful **general strike** launched in U.S. history. It brought a major city to a halt.

During the 1920s, the stock market rose, and products such as radios and automobiles became available to the average consumer. But in 1929, the Great Depression hit. It was the worst economic downturn in the nation's history. The Depression gripped the United States throughout the 1930s. Millions of people lost their jobs, and many people could not pay their bills. Many were homeless and hungry. In the deepest days of the Depression, one out of three Washington factory workers was jobless, and many of the state's lumber mills shut down.

"SOLIDARITY FOREVER"

The Wobblies are remembered for their spirited fights for laborers and for their songs such as "**Solidarity** Forever," which is sung to the tune of "Battle Hymn of the Republic."

> When the Union's inspiration through the workers' blood shall run,
> There can be no power greater anywhere beneath the sun.
> Yet what force on earth is weaker than the feeble strength of one?
> For the Union makes us strong.
> Solidarity forever, Solidarity forever, Solidarity forever
> For the Union makes us strong.

WORDS TO KNOW

solidarity *unity that is based on shared interests or goals*

general strike *an organized refusal to work by all workers in a city or region*

Bertha Knight Landes was elected mayor of Seattle in 1926. She was the first woman to be elected mayor of a large American city.

President Franklin Roosevelt started a series of programs called the New Deal to put people back to work. Among the most ambitious projects was the construction of a series of dams on the Columbia River. Work on the Bonneville Dam began in 1933 near Vancouver. The Bonneville Dam generated electricity and helped make the Columbia River navigable for boat traffic. An even larger building project was the Grand Coulee Dam, northwest of Spokane. Some 7,000 laborers worked on this dam. When it was completed in 1942, the Grand Coulee was the largest concrete dam in North America and one of the greatest single sources of electricity in the world.

WORLD WAR II

On December 7, 1941, Japanese airplanes bombed Pearl Harbor in Hawai'i, plunging the nation into World War II. Fear gripped Washington and the entire West Coast in the months following Pearl Harbor. Americans believed Japanese forces were poised to invade and occupy California, Oregon, and Washington. Many Americans heard rumors that Japanese Americans were plotting to help the enemy take over the coastal areas.

Responding to this fear, President Franklin Roosevelt issued an order forcing all residents of Japanese heritage to move from the West Coast. In all, 110,000 Japanese Americans, 14,000 from Washington, were relocated to what were called internment camps, far from the Pacific Coast. The internment camps were built inland in dry, dusty regions. They were ringed by barbed wire and guarded by soldiers carrying rifles.

People of Japanese ancestry were confined to these camps for most of the wartime years, even though most were citizens of the United States. Some young men from these camps volunteered to fight for their country. Their

FAQ

Q8 HOW MUCH CONCRETE WENT INTO THE GRAND COULEE DAM?

A8 Enough concrete was poured into the Grand Coulee to build a two-lane highway running from Seattle to New York City.

Japanese Americans line up for a meal at an internment camp in Puyallup, June 1942.

442nd Infantry Regiment won many battles in Italy and earned more medals for bravery than any other U.S. unit.

Japanese Americans suffered during World War II largely because they were not protected by law. The law at the time denied full citizenship privileges to Asians, especially those not born in the United States. European Americans feared competition for jobs and pressed politicians to pass laws against Japanese newcomers. Starting in 1907, an agreement between the United States and Japan restricted Japanese laborers from coming into the country. The Immigration Act of 1924 banned all immigration from Japan. In 1952, the law was finally changed to allow limited Japanese immigration and to allow Japanese immigrants to become full U.S. citizens.

GALLOPING GERTIE

The Tacoma Narrows Bridge opened on July 1, 1940, and stretched from Tacoma to Kitsap Peninsula. The bridge swayed and vibrated, earning the nickname Galloping Gertie. Just a few months later, on the windy morning of November 7, the bridge collapsed into Puget Sound. The collapse was captured on film and has become a classic example of engineering failure. No human life was lost, but a dog was trapped in a car and died. Today, two Tacoma Narrows Bridges, with improved designs, stand in the same spot as the original bridge.

TAKUJI YAMASHITA: FIGHTING FOR RIGHTS

Takuji Yamashita (1874–1959) was born in Japan and came to the United States in the 1890s. He graduated from the University of Washington's law school but was denied permission to practice law because of his Japanese heritage. Several times, Yamashita went to court to challenge this restriction and obtain a law license. He lost all challenges. At the start of World War II, he and his family were interned, and they lost what had been a thriving hotel business. In 1957, Yamashita went back to Japan, where he died two years later. In 2001, 99 years after he graduated from law school and long after he was dead, Yamashita was granted an honorary license to practice law in Washington.

? Want to know more? Visit www.factsfornow .scholastic.com and enter the keyword **Washington**.

The demands of war spurred the Washington economy. Thousands worked in the shipyards of Seattle, Tacoma, Bremerton, Vancouver, and Grays Harbor. The Boeing Airplane Company of Seattle grew explosively. Boeing engineers designed the B-17 and the B-29, the two most powerful U.S. bombers of the war. More than 50,000 men and women worked in the Boeing plants.

A top secret project grew at a place called Hanford near the town of Richland. Before the war ended, 50,000 people lived in Hanford, making it the fifth-largest city in the

Workers construct B-17 F bombers at the Boeing plant in Seattle, November 1942.

We Can Do It!

POST FEB. 15 TO FEB. 28

WAR PRODUCTION CO-ORDINATING COMMITTEE

WOMEN AT WORK

Before World War II, few women worked in factories. They were considered too delicate to handle the heavy work. But during the war, so many men had joined the military that factory owners were forced to hire women. Women soon outnumbered men in aircraft plants and shipyards. These women were vital to the war effort. One fictional factory worker was pictured on wartime posters flexing her muscles and exclaiming, "We can do it!"

state. Only a handful of the residents knew they were engaged in making plutonium, a material vital for building the atomic bomb.

Japan surrendered on August 14, 1945, shortly after atomic bombs destroyed the Japanese cities of Hiroshima and Nagasaki. The bombs were dropped by B-29 bombers, designed by Boeing engineers in Seattle. The Nagasaki bomb was made from plutonium enriched at the plant in Hanford, Washington.

Boeing B-52

MODERN WASHINGTON

During the war years, thousands of people went to Washington seeking industrial jobs. Many decided to stay in the Evergreen State after the war ended. The state's population increased from 1.7 million in 1940 to nearly 2.4 million in 1950. Washington also grew more diverse. The African American population increased from 7,000 to 30,000 during the 1940s. The Hispanic population also increased dramatically, rising from about 2,400 in 1940 to more than 70,000 by 1970.

The 1950s was a prosperous time for Washington. Seattle's Boeing Company pioneered the development of passenger jets such as the 707. Boeing also built the B-52 bomber, which is still being used by the U.S. Air Force. During the 1950s, many Washington families moved from the cities to the suburbs. The Puget Sound area led the way. Bellevue grew from a sleepy farming village into the leading suburb of Seattle. The towns of Kent and Federal Way blossomed from what had been farmers' fields.

The Seattle World's Fair, officially called the Century 21 Exposition, opened in 1962. The fair lasted six months and attracted more than 9 million visitors. Century 21 changed Seattle's skyline by giving it the futuristic Space Needle. In 1967, the I-5 freeway was completed, linking the Columbia River with Canada. Also the National Basketball Association's Seattle SuperSonics arrived to give the state its first major sports franchise.

In the 1960s, as racial tensions increased in the state's major cities, citizens of all backgrounds wanted to do something positive. Laws were passed that banned **discrimination** in housing. Since 1975, African Americans have been elected mayors of Seattle, Spokane, and Roslyn, and others have served in city councils, school boards, and the legislature.

WORD TO KNOW

discrimination *unequal treatment based on race, gender, religion, or other factors*

The Space Needle was added to the Seattle skyline as part of the 1962 world's fair.

In the 1960s, many Washingtonians grew more concerned with the pollution of the environment. Years of logging and industrial development had felled forests and polluted rivers and lakes. Lake Washington, a playground for people in the Seattle area, had become so foul that swimming was banned. With great effort, the state constructed sewage disposal plants, and Lake Washington was cleaned up. Pollution was reduced in the Spokane River in time for the city of Spokane's world's fair in 1974, which helped revitalize downtown Spokane. Logging was also restricted to preserve the state's old-growth trees.

MINI-BIO

JANET MCCLOUD: DEFENDING NATIVE RIGHTS

A Tulalip woman named Janet McCloud (1934–2003) rose to the defense of her people when state government officials violated their salmon fishing rights. In 1961, two of her brothers-in-law were arrested for fishing, so McCloud and other Native American women took up fishing as a protest. The men were released, and McCloud organized the Survival of American Indians Association. She went on to work for better Indian education, preservation of Native languages and culture, and the rights of Indians in jail.

? **Want to know more?** Visit www.factsfornow .scholastic.com and enter the keyword **Washington**.

Q8 WAS ANYONE KILLED IN THE MOUNT ST. HELENS ERUPTION?

A8 Yes, at least 57 people who lived near the mountain lost their lives.

As part of Washington's efforts to preserve the environment, the government restricted the fishing rights of Native Americans. In treaties in the 1850s, Native Americans of the Pacific Northwest had given up 40 million acres (16 million ha) of land in exchange for the right to fish in their traditional fishing places. But by the middle of the 20th century, state game wardens were arresting Indians for fishing. Native Americans sometimes held "fish-ins," in which they would set up fishing camps and fish as a protest and to attract attention to their cause. They also filed suit in court arguing that their treaty rights were being violated. In 1974, Judge George Boldt decided in favor of the Native Americans, guaranteeing them the right to fish.

In a spectacular demonstration of the power of nature, Mount St. Helens erupted on May 18, 1980. For months, the mountain had been rumbling as if to give warning of the event to come, but few were prepared for the violent force of this eruption. The top of Mount St. Helens blew off, and white ash spewed out of the volcano, turning midday into darkness.

In the late 20th century, the Boeing Company continued to be the state's largest private employer. Some leaders worried that Washington had become overly dependent on Boeing and that a slowdown in the aircraft business could throw the entire state into a depression. Then a Seattle native named Bill Gates came to the rescue. Along

Microsoft

with his business partner, Paul Allen, Gates cofounded the Microsoft Corporation and created some of the most widely used computer software in history. The company quickly became a major employer in Washington.

In 2013, several underground tanks at the Hanford nuclear production site were found to be leaking radioactive waste. Reports about radioactivity released at Hanford have been issued since the 1960s, but the new discoveries caused residents great alarm. The U.S. government has spent billions of dollars to clean up the site, but progress has been slow. Today, Washingtonians continue to face the challenge of encouraging economic growth while at the same time protecting the environment and quality of life that attract so many people to their state.

Microsoft continues to produce some of the world's most-used computer software and hardware.

70

Hikers enjoy the
sights at Mount
Rainier National Park.

PEOPLE

★

WASHINGTONIANS TAKE PRIDE IN THEIR STATE'S BEAUTY. And most residents like nothing better than heading outdoors to enjoy it. They go hiking, biking, fishing, and sailing. They explore dark caves and damp forests. Because of Washington's varied terrain, a Washingtonian can start the day skiing in the Cascades, and then take a drive and cap off the evening with a swim in the Pacific Ocean.

WASHINGTON RESIDENTS

In 2010, the U.S. Census counted 6,724,540 residents of Washington, an increase of more than 14 percent since 2000. Most of the increase was a result of net migration, meaning more people moved to Washington than left the state. By every measure, Washington is a growing state.

The majority of Washington's residents are of European descent. They are most likely to be of German, English, Irish, Scandinavian, French, or Italian heritage. Hispanics, most of whom are of Mexican descent, make up more than 11 percent of the population. Asian Americans make up just over 7 percent of the population. The largest group of Asians in Washington trace their ancestry to the Philippines. Most of the 3.4 percent of Washingtonians who are African American live in the Seattle-Tacoma area.

WOW

The nation's first Father's Day was celebrated on June 19, 1910. The idea to have a special day honoring American fathers came from Sonora Louise Smart Dodd of Spokane.

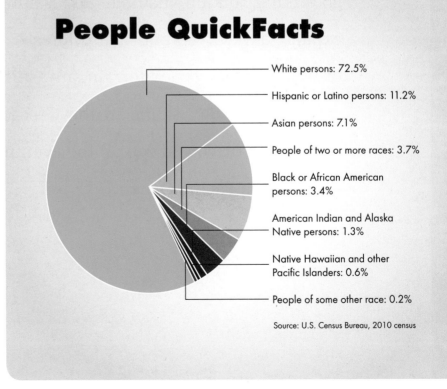

People QuickFacts

White persons: 72.5%

Hispanic or Latino persons: 11.2%

Asian persons: 7.1%

People of two or more races: 3.7%

Black or African American persons: 3.4%

American Indian and Alaska Native persons: 1.3%

Native Hawaiian and other Pacific Islanders: 0.6%

People of some other race: 0.2%

Source: U.S. Census Bureau, 2010 census

A large number of Native Americans live in Washington, many on the 27 reservations scattered throughout the state. The largest groups are Yakamas, Colvilles, Lummis, Tulalips, Spokanes, and Puyallups.

CITY LIFE AND COUNTRY LIFE

Around 84 percent of Washingtonians live in cities and towns, most of them west of the Cascades. The cities of Seattle, Tacoma, and Bellevue—all in the Puget Sound region—account for about half the state's population.

The vast region east of the Cascades is sometimes called Washington's Inland Empire. The east is mostly

Where Washingtonians Live

The colors on this map indicate population density throughout the state. The darker the color, the more people live there.

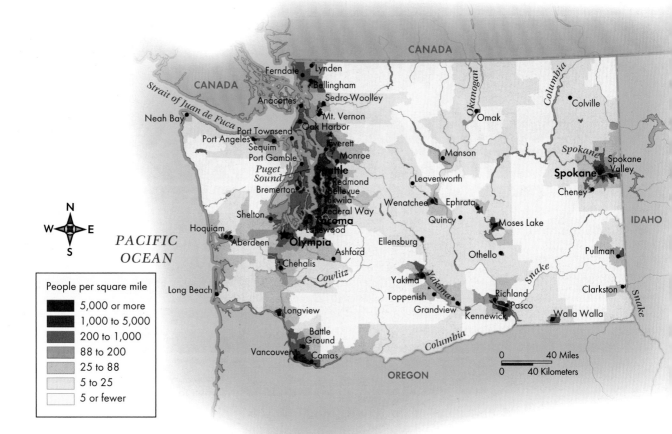

People per square mile

- 5,000 or more
- 1,000 to 5,000
- 200 to 1,000
- 88 to 200
- 25 to 88
- 5 to 25
- 5 or fewer

Big City Life

This list shows the population of Washington's biggest cities.

Seattle	608,660
Spokane	208,916
Tacoma	198,397
Vancouver	161,791
Bellevue	122,363

Source: U.S. Census Bureau, 2010 census

farmland and is sparsely populated compared to the west. The exceptions to this pattern are Spokane—the largest city in the eastern part of the state and the second-largest city in the entire state—and the Tri-City region of Richland, Kennewick, and Pasco.

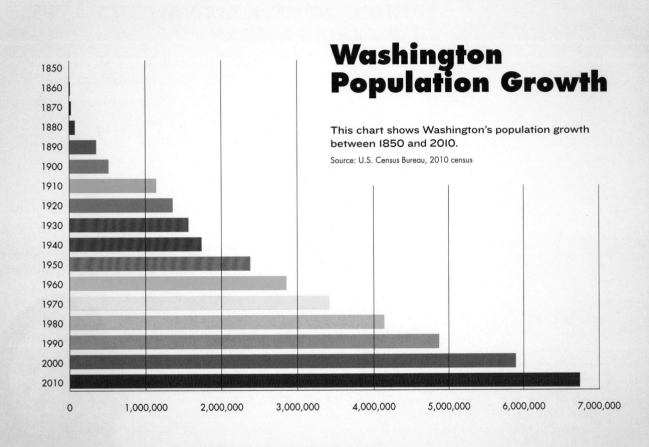

Washington Population Growth

This chart shows Washington's population growth between 1850 and 2010.

Source: U.S. Census Bureau, 2010 census

In pioneer days, Washington was overwhelmingly rural. Not until the late 1800s did cities begin to grow. Now most Washingtonians live and work in urban areas. In the cities, people have close access to schools, libraries, shopping, and cultural institutions such as theaters and museums. But residents of metropolitan Seattle complain their highways are constantly jammed with traffic. Highways are less crowded in the farm areas. Rural ways of life have changed, but many farm traditions remain strong. Most people who live in rural Washington work in farm-related businesses or in the forest industry.

HOW TO TALK LIKE A WASHINGTONIAN

Do you want to talk like a Washingtonian? Then carry water in a "bucket" rather than a "pail," drink a "pop" with lunch instead of a "soda," and call the chips of bark you use to landscape your yard "beauty bark."

HOW TO EAT LIKE A WASHINGTONIAN

Western Washington is bound by coastline, and the state's restaurants have long served some of the country's finest and freshest seafood. Some restaurants combine Washington's fish dishes with produce from the state's fruit farms. Try salmon in blackberry sauce—it's a treat. In cities, you can enjoy food from around the world, including Chinese, Japanese, Filipino, and Indian. Seattle is known for its marvelous Mexican restaurants.

Shopping for apples at a farmers' market

FARMERS' MARKETS

Farmers' markets operate in most of Washington's small towns, often on Saturday mornings. The open-air markets give farmers an opportunity to sell their produce directly to customers. People enjoy the markets because the produce they buy there is completely fresh. Farmers' markets also give residents the opportunity to get together and chat. The state government encourages the markets and maintains a Web site (www.wafarmersmarkets.com) that provides a list of the active farmers' markets operating in Washington.

MENU

WHAT'S ON THE MENU IN WASHINGTON?

★ ★ ★

Cedar plank salmon

Cedar Plank Salmon

Native people feasted on salmon thousands of years ago, and it is still a favorite among Washingtonians today. A popular way to prepare it is to barbecue it on a piece of cedar that has been soaked in salt.

Razor Clams

Washingtonians dig up these tasty clams on the state's sandy beaches. They eat them breaded and fried.

Chicken Teriyaki

This dish of chicken cooked in a sweet soy sauce was inspired by Japanese cooking.

Blackberry Pie

Blackberries grow wild in Washington, and blackberry pie is a delicious summertime treat.

TRY THIS RECIPE
Apple Brown Betty

Washington is the country's biggest producer of apples. Washingtonians are proud of this title, and apples are used in dozens of dishes in the state. Cooks prepare apple fritters, apple pie, apple cake, apple cobbler, apple crisp, apple dumplings, and dozens more such delights. One of the state's favorites is a dessert called apple brown betty. Have an adult nearby when you make this recipe.

Ingredients:
3 medium apples
6 tablespoons unsalted butter, melted
1½ cups bread crumbs
1¼ cups packed brown sugar
1 teaspoon cinnamon
¼ teaspoon nutmeg
3 tablespoons lemon juice
Ice cream or whipped cream

Instructions:
1. Preheat the oven to 350°F.
2. Peel, core, and slice the apples.
3. In a small bowl, stir together the melted butter and bread crumbs.
4. In another bowl, stir together the brown sugar, cinnamon, and nutmeg.
5. Spread one-third of the crumb mixture across the bottom of a 9-inch pie pan. Cover this mixture with half the apples and then sprinkle with half the sugar mixture. Sprinkle 1½ tablespoons of the lemon juice across the top.
6. Add another one-third of the crumb mixture, the rest of the apples, and the rest of the sugar mixture. Sprinkle on the remaining 1½ tablespoons of lemon juice. Finally, top with the remaining crumb mixture.
7. Cover the pie pan with foil and bake about 40 minutes, or until the apples are tender. Then remove the foil, raise the temperature to 400°F, and bake another 15 minutes, to "brown" the betty.
8. Serve with ice cream or whipped cream.

Apple brown betty

On campus at the University of Washington in Seattle

GEOGRAPHY WIZARDS

Every year, some 5 million students from around the nation compete in the National Geographic Bee. In 2007, Caitlin Snaring, an eighth-grader from Redmond, Washington, won the contest and received $25,000 in college scholarship funds. Caitlin was the fifth student from Washington to capture top honors at the geography bee. No other state has produced as many winners.

EDUCATION

Whitman College, founded in 1859 at Walla Walla, was Washington's first institution of higher learning. The University of Washington in Seattle and Washington State University in Pullman are the largest public universities in the state. The University of Washington is home to one of the country's leading medical schools and nursing schools. It also has highly ranked programs in education, engineering, and computer science. Major private colleges include Gonzaga University in Spokane, the University of Puget Sound in Tacoma, Seattle Pacific University, and Seattle University.

ART AND MUSIC

The art world in Washington reflects the state's diverse history. The Seattle Art Museum has a renowned collection of Asian art. An excellent selection of Native American art and crafts are displayed at Eastern Washington State Historical Society and Museum in Spokane. Many leading artists, including Robert Motherwell, Chuck Close, and Jacob Lawrence, have made their homes in Washington. One of the state's most prominent artists today is Dale Chihuly, who makes colorful objects from blown glass. Chihuly designed a glass footbridge in his hometown of Tacoma. Many other glass artists also work in west-

Artist Chuck Close at an exhibition of his photographs in New York City

JACOB LAWRENCE: PAINTER

Jacob Lawrence (1917–2000) was an artist who often used bold colors and forms to depict African American history and culture. He was born in New Jersey and as a teenager moved to Harlem, a predominantly African American neighborhood in New York City. Harlem had a thriving artistic community, and Lawrence trained there to be an artist. When he was in his 20s, he began a series of paintings that portrayed black life during the Great Migration period, when hundreds of thousands of African Americans moved to northern states. By 1971, Lawrence had settled in Seattle, where he became an art professor. He created paintings depicting the life of pioneer George Washington Bush, some of which now hang at the Washington State History Museum in Tacoma.

? Want to know more? Visit www.factsfornow .scholastic.com and enter the keyword **Washington**.

MINI-BIO

KURT COBAIN: ROCK LEGEND

Kurt Cobain (1967–1994) grew up in the logging town of Aberdeen. At age four, he began singing and playing piano and soon developed an interest in a broad range of musical styles. In 1987, he formed the band Nirvana with bassist Krist Novoselic, later adding drummer Dave Grohl to the lineup. The band often performed in Olympia during its early days. They achieved massive, worldwide popularity with the release of their 1991 album *Nevermind*. Sadly, Cobain had difficulty coping with the band's sudden success and committed suicide in 1994. However, his music has lived on, and Nirvana remains one of the best-loved bands in rock history. In 2014, the group was inducted into the Rock and Roll Hall of Fame.

Want to know more? Visit www.factsfornow .scholastic.com and enter the keyword **Washington**.

ern Washington. Many of their works are on display at Tacoma's Museum of Glass.

In the 1960s, Seattle-born rock star Jimi Hendrix stunned audiences with his inventive guitar playing. In the 1980s and 1990s, Seattle was the center of the "grunge" music scene, the home of leading bands such as Nirvana and Pearl Jam.

WRITERS

Many acclaimed writers have hailed from Washington. Mary McCarthy, who was born in Seattle, lived in New York as an adult and wrote about the people

Poet and short-story writer Raymond Carver grew up in Yakima.

she encountered there. Her most widely read novel, *The Group* (1963), concerns young college women entering the adult world in the 1930s. Frank Herbert wrote about worlds even farther from Washington. His 1965 novel *Dune* takes place on a desert planet inhabited by giant worms.

Other writers often reflect their experiences in Washington in their work. Carlos Bulosan was a teenager when he moved to Seattle from the Philippines, and he drew on his experiences as a migrant laborer and cannery worker in books such as *America Is in the Heart.* Short-story writer Raymond Carver grew up in a working-class family in Yakima. His story collection *Will You Please Be Quiet, Please?* is populated by people from the Northwest struggling with life. Carver was also an accomplished poet. Gary Snyder is a poet whose work expresses his concern for the environment and interest in Native American and Asian cultures and religions. Sherman Alexie, who was born on the Spokane Indian Reservation, also drew on his own experiences to write books such as *Reservation Blues.* Randall Beth Platt's young adult novel *The Likes of Me* tells the story of an

MINI-BIO

SHERMAN ALEXIE: AWARD-WINNING WRITER

Sherman Alexie (1966–) was born on the Spokane Indian Reservation. He suffered from a serious illness at birth, and doctors feared he would be mentally disabled. But he soon proved them wrong, learning to read at age three. When Alexie entered Washington State University, he intended to become a doctor, but he switched to writing poetry and stories. His first book, a collection of stories called *The Business of Fancydancing,* was published in 1991. This and later works, such as *The Lone Ranger and Tonto Fistfight in Heaven* and *Reservation Blues,* reflect his Native American background. In 2007, Alexie won the National Book Award for best young-adult novel for *The Absolutely True Diary of a Part-Time Indian,* about a teenage boy who decides to leave the reservation school for a "white" school.

? **Want to know more?** Visit www.factsfornow.scholastic.com and enter the keyword **Washington**.

albino girl growing up in a northwestern Washington logging community in 1918 with her father and her stepmother, who is nearly 7 feet (213 cm) tall.

SPORTS AND OUTDOOR ACTIVITIES

Washington is a wonderland for those who love the outdoors. The state has three national parks—Mount Rainier, North Cascades, and Olympic. Washington also has six national forests lying wholly within its borders, two other national forests that it shares with neighboring states, and many national recreation areas. Washington also has more than 140 state parks.

Hiking trails and bike paths lace every section of the state's wilderness areas. The popular and rugged Dog Mountain Trail winds along the Columbia River near the town of Stevenson. Hikers who climb the steep trail are often rewarded with sights of beautiful wildflowers. More

Hikers in the Cascade Mountains

Seahawks quarterback Russell Wilson celebrates the team's Super Bowl victory in 2014.

than 600 miles (966 km) of hiking trails crisscross Olympic National Park. Hiking is the best way to tour the park, because cars frighten wildlife. Walk the trails and you might spot one of the park's many herds of Roosevelt elk.

Washington's major league sports teams are all based in Seattle. Baseball fans cheer on the Mariners, and football fans root for the Seahawks, who won the Super Bowl for the first time in 2014. Many basketball fans were disappointed to see the SuperSonics leave Washington in 2008, but they cheer the WNBA Seattle Storm.

College sports are also popular, especially football. One day each November, when the University of Washington Huskies of Seattle play the Washington State Cougars, streets across the state are quiet because most Washingtonians are planted in front of their TVs, watching this clash between rivals.

READ ABOUT

Governor Jay Inslee meets with voters during his 2012 campaign.

GOVERNMENT

CHAPTER SEVEN

★

WHY DO CITIZENS NEED AN ORGANIZED GOVERNMENT? A government provides services and brings order to a community. The government maintains roads, protects the environment, funds libraries, and provides police and fire protection. In Washington, the government also runs a large public school system, one of the country's best. Government benefits all Washingtonians, including the youngest residents.

THE CAPITAL

Olympia has been the capital of Washington since territorial times. The governor's mansion, the supreme court building, and the capitol all sit in a park next to Capitol Lake. The capitol, which has an imposing dome, dominates the area.

THE CONSTITUTION

A constitution is a written set of laws and rules that everyone—government officials as well as individual citizens—must follow. Washington's constitution was written in 1889, the year it became a state. Over the years, that constitution has been amended (changed) many times. The constitution divides state government into three parts: the executive branch, which carries out laws; the legislative branch, which creates new laws and **rescinds** old ones; and the judicial branch, which tries cases and interprets the constitution.

WORD TO KNOW

rescinds *declares null and void*

The capitol in Olympia

Capital City

This map shows places of interest in Olympia, Washington's capital city.

CAPITOL FACTS

Here are some fascinating facts about Washington's state capitol:

- The building is made of 173 million pounds (78 million kilograms) of stone, brick, concrete, and steel.
- When completed in 1928, its final cost was $7,385,768; if it were built with the same materials and the same workmanship today, its cost would be $1 billion.
- It has survived three earthquakes, including a severe one in 1949.
- The building is 287 feet (87 m) high, making it the fourth-tallest masonry dome in the world.

In 1910, Washington became the fifth state to grant women the right to vote. Ten years later, the 19th Amendment to the U.S. Constitution granted all women in the nation the right to vote.

EXECUTIVE BRANCH

Washington's executive branch is headed by a governor and a lieutenant governor, both of whom are elected to four-year terms. The governor appoints the heads of many agencies and departments. He or she also recommends a budget and makes

SEE IT HERE!

OLYMPIA'S JAPANESE GARDENS

In 1981, Washington's capital city of Olympia became the sister city of the town of Yashiro, Japan, which is now called Kato City. Groups from the two cities have exchanged visits, establishing enduring friendships. In 1989, in downtown Olympia, the Yashiro Japanese Garden opened, representing that friendship. The lovely garden contains lanterns, a waterfall, and a bamboo grove.

Washington State Government

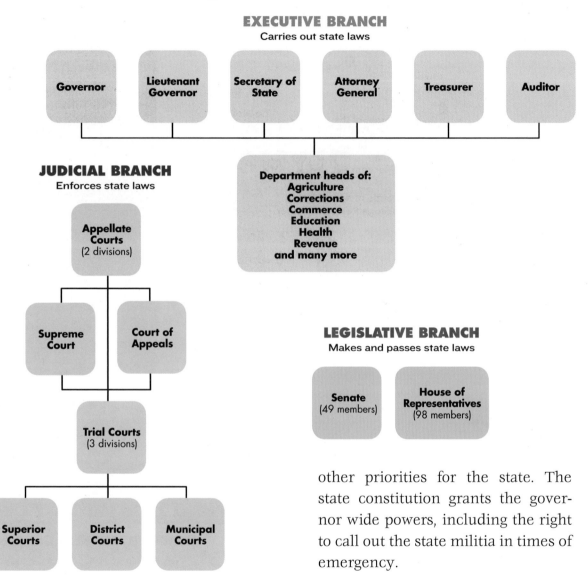

EXECUTIVE BRANCH
Carries out state laws

Governor

Lieutenant Governor

Secretary of State

Attorney General

Treasurer

Auditor

JUDICIAL BRANCH
Enforces state laws

Department heads of:
Agriculture
Corrections
Commerce
Education
Health
Revenue
and many more

Appellate Courts
(2 divisions)

Supreme Court

Court of Appeals

LEGISLATIVE BRANCH
Makes and passes state laws

Senate
(49 members)

House of Representatives
(98 members)

Trial Courts
(3 divisions)

Superior Courts

District Courts

Municipal Courts

WORDS TO KNOW

auditor *someone who checks financial accounts*

attorney general *chief legal adviser and law officer*

other priorities for the state. The state constitution grants the governor wide powers, including the right to call out the state militia in times of emergency.

The lieutenant governor takes over if the governor is unable to perform his or her duties. Other elected officials who serve in the executive branch include the **auditor**, the **attorney general**, and the treasurer.

Washington Senate Majority Leader Rodney Tom discusses a new law with his fellow senators in 2014.

LEGISLATIVE BRANCH

Washington's legislature is made up of two houses, a senate and a house of representatives. The state is divided into 49 legislative districts. Voters in each district elect one senator and two representatives. Senators serve four-year terms, and representatives serve two-year terms. Members of both houses discuss proposed laws, called bills. After both houses pass a bill, it is sent to the governor for his or her final approval. When the governor signs the bill, it becomes law. A governor may veto, or refuse to sign, a bill. The legislature can override a veto by repassing the bill with a two-thirds majority of both houses. The bill then becomes law despite the governor's wishes.

MINI-BIO

GARY LOCKE: PIONEERING GOVERNOR

Gary Locke (1950–) was born in Seattle and grew up working in the grocery store owned by his immigrant parents. Locke entered politics in 1982 when he was elected to the Washington House of Representatives, where he earned a reputation as a hard worker who immersed himself in the details of policies. In 1996, he was elected governor of Washington, making him the first Chinese American governor of any U.S. state and the first Asian American governor outside of Hawai'i. From 2009 to 2011, Locke served in the administration of President Barack Obama as the U.S. Secretary of Commerce. In 2011, Obama appointed him the U.S. ambassador to China, a position he occupied until early 2014.

 Want to know more? Visit www.facts fornow.scholastic.com and enter the keyword **Washington**.

Washington was the first state to have women serving as governor (Christine Gregoire) and both U.S. senators (Patty Murray and Maria Cantwell) at the same time.

MINI-BIO

PHYLLIS GUTIÉRREZ KENNEY: GROUNDBREAKING LEGISLATOR

Phyllis Gutiérrez Kenney (1936—) was born in Harden, Montana, to migrant-farmworker parents. She and her seven siblings traveled from state-to-state harvesting the crops before settling in Wapato, Washington. Representative Gutiérrez Kenney has dedicated herself in service to her community and Latinos throughout Washington State. In her professional career, she co-founded the Washington State Migrant Child Care centers, founded the Educational Institute for Rural Families, and helped establish the Farm Worker Health Clinics in Washington. Though she retired from government in 2012, she continues to be a strong advocate for education, children's health care, and equal rights for all Washingtonians.

? Want to know more? Visit www.factsfornow .scholastic.com and enter the keyword **Washington**.

Representing Washington

This list shows the number of elected officials who represent Washington, both on the state and national levels.

OFFICE	NUMBER	LENGTH OF TERM
State senators	49	4 years
State representatives	98	2 years
U.S. senators	2	6 years
U.S. representatives	10	2 years
Presidential electors	12	—

JUDICIAL BRANCH

The judicial branch is made up of the state's court system. Each county in Washington has a district court, which hears cases involving minor crimes and lawsuits. Each county also has a superior court, which handles more serious criminal and civil cases. Judges on both superior and district courts are elected to four-year terms.

Someone who believes a superior court made a mistake during a case can have the state court of appeals review the decision. Judges on the court of appeals are elected to six-year terms.

The state's highest court is the supreme court, which has nine judges who are elected to six-year terms. The judges choose one of their members to be the chief justice. The supreme court reviews decisions made by the state court of appeals.

Justices of the Washington State Supreme Court meet with members of the state legislature.

TOM FOLEY: DEDICATED PUBLIC SERVANT

Thomas Foley (1929–2013), a native of Spokane and graduate of the University of Washington, served for 30 years (1965–1995) as a Democratic member of the U.S. House of Representatives. He was the Speaker of the House, the chamber's presiding officer, from 1989 to 1995. In 1997, President Bill Clinton appointed Foley the U.S. ambassador to Japan, a position he held until 2001. Two years later, Foley was awarded the Washington Medal of Merit, the state's highest honor, for his outstanding service to Washingtonians.

? **Want to know more?** Visit www.factsfor now.scholastic.com and enter the keyword **Washington**.

Washington's smallest incorporated city is the town of Krupp, in the east-central part of the state. In 2010, Krupp had a population of 48.

Washington Counties

This map shows the 39 counties in Washington. Olympia, the state capital, is indicated with a star.

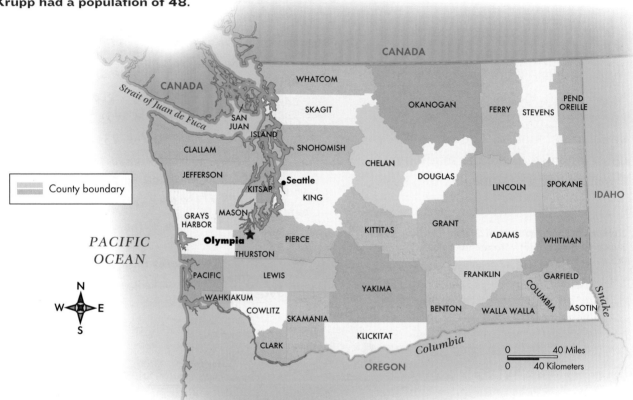

KIDS RULE

You must be 18 or older to vote in Washington. But that restriction does not mean children have no voice in the state's decisions. For many years, Washington leaders have asked schoolchildren to choose state symbols. In 1997, after a group of students from the city of Kent brought the idea to the legislature, children from 100 school districts statewide elected the green darner dragonfly the state insect. Thanks to the kids of the Windsor Elementary School near Cheney, the Columbian mammoth is the state fossil. Ten thousand years ago, Columbian mammoths roamed the Pacific Northwest, and their remains have been found on the Olympic Peninsula. Children are also responsible for the legislature selecting the orca as the state marine mammal and the Pacific chorus frog as the state amphibian.

Members of the Seattle City Council attend a meeting in 2014.

LOCAL GOVERNMENT

Washington has 39 counties and nearly 300 **incorporated** cities and towns. These local governments provide road maintenance, police, schools, and other vital services for their communities. Most of Washington's towns are run by a mayor and a city council.

WORD TO KNOW

incorporated *recognized as a self-governing organization*

State Flag

Adopted in 1923, the flag shows the state seal against a dark green background. Prior to 1923, Washington had no official flag.

State Seal

The state seal shows a picture of George Washington based on a portrait painted by Gilbert Stuart in 1796. Around the portrait is a circle of gold that contains the words "The Seal of the State of Washington" and "1889," the year Washington became a state. The secretary of state still uses the 1889 die and press to impress the seal on official state documents.

READ ABOUT

A Microsoft employee demonstrates features of the company's Windows 8 operating system.

CHAPTER EIGHT

ECONOMY

★

IN THE 1800s, WASHINGTON'S ECONOMY WAS BASED ON FARMING, LOGGING, AND FISHING. Those three industries are still important to the state, but now Washington's economy has developed beyond anything the pioneers could have imagined. Washington workers now design computer programs that help you find information in a flash and build rockets that zoom into space.

DOING THINGS FOR OTHERS

Most Washingtonians work in the service industry and make no products at all. Service workers provide their customers with services rather than making or growing products. The nurse who checks your blood pressure, the clerk who sells you a video game, and the person who teaches karate are all service workers. So are teachers and police officers, architects and lawyers, and waiters and cooks.

What Do Washingtonians Do?

This color-coded chart shows what industries Washingtonians work in.

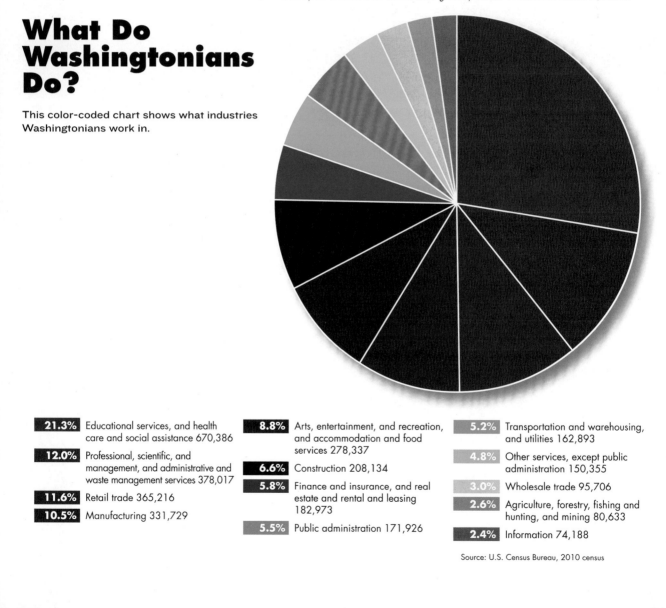

21.3% Educational services, and health care and social assistance 670,386

12.0% Professional, scientific, and management, and administrative and waste management services 378,017

11.6% Retail trade 365,216

10.5% Manufacturing 331,729

8.8% Arts, entertainment, and recreation, and accommodation and food services 278,337

6.6% Construction 208,134

5.8% Finance and insurance, and real estate and rental and leasing 182,973

5.5% Public administration 171,926

5.2% Transportation and warehousing, and utilities 162,893

4.8% Other services, except public administration 150,355

3.0% Wholesale trade 95,706

2.6% Agriculture, forestry, fishing and hunting, and mining 80,633

2.4% Information 74,188

Source: U.S. Census Bureau, 2010 census

Police officers are among the many service workers in the state of Washington.

Finance and real estate are among the state's leading economic activities, and both are service industries. Insurance is another important service business. Washington's bankers, insurance representatives, and real estate agents all play a part in the economy.

The Cascade Range, which separates Washington into two climate zones, also divides the state's agriculture. Dairy farms are found in the wetter regions west of the Cascades, whereas sheep ranches are common in the drier east. Beef cattle are also raised in the eastern regions. In the 20th century, dams were built on the Columbia River. These dams enable farmers to use the river water to irrigate their fields. Valleys in Central Washington, east of the Cascades, are now highly productive because of irrigation.

Washington ranks second only to Idaho in the production of potatoes.

Harvesting apples, one of Washington's most important crops

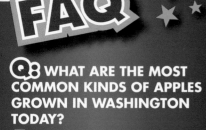

FAQ

Q8 WHAT ARE THE MOST COMMON KINDS OF APPLES GROWN IN WASHINGTON TODAY?

A8 The most common types are red delicious, Fuji, and gala apples.

More than half of the apples consumed in the United States come from Washington. The state also exports apples to dozens of foreign countries.

Apples, the symbol of Washington, are the state's most important agricultural crop. The grape and wine industries add more than $8.5 billion to the state's economy each year, while employing roughly 30,000 people. Large growing regions are found in the Yakima Valley, the Walla Walla Valley, and the Columbia Valley. The state also produces other fruits, including cherries and plums.

MADE IN WASHINGTON

Every year, Washington factories produce goods worth billions of dollars. Transportation equipment, which includes aircraft and ships, leads the state's manufacturing sector. Boeing, which employs more Washingtonians than any other company, has huge aircraft manufacturing plants in the Puget Sound area. Shipyards at Bremerton, Seattle, and Tacoma build vessels of all shapes and sizes.

Computers and electronics equipment are Washington's second-largest manufacturing enterprises. The computer giant Microsoft is headquartered in Redmond, near Seattle, and employs thousands of Washingtonians. Other companies produce computer microchips, medical equipment, and navigational instruments for airplanes and ships.

SEE IT HERE!

GEORGE, WASHINGTON

The tiny town of George—yes, there is a George, Washington—lies in a fruit-growing region in the eastern part of the state. Since President George Washington is so closely associated with the cherry tree, the people of his namesake town celebrate that fruit. Every Fourth of July, the residents bake what they call the world's largest cherry pie. Streets in George are named after varieties of cherries such as Bing Avenue and Maraschino Avenue.

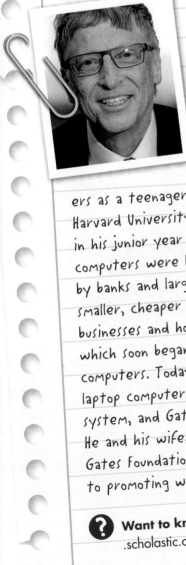

MINI-BIO

BILL GATES: CHANGING THE WORLD

William "Bill" Gates (1955–) grew up in Seattle and developed a passionate interest in computers as a teenager. In 1973, Gates began college at Harvard University in Massachusetts, but dropped out in his junior year to pursue a dream. At the time, computers were large, expensive devices used mainly by banks and large corporations. He envisioned making smaller, cheaper computers that could be used in small businesses and homes. In 1975, he founded Microsoft, which soon began producing software for personal computers. Today, most of the world's desktop and laptop computers use a Microsoft Windows operating system, and Gates is one of the world's richest men. He and his wife, Melinda, direct the Bill & Melinda Gates Foundation, which funds organizations dedicated to promoting world health.

? **Want to know more?** Visit www.factsfornow .scholastic.com and enter the keyword **Washington**.

Major Agricultural and Mining Products

This map shows where Washington's major agricultural and mining products come from. See a cow? That means cattle are found there.

Food processing is another leading industry in Washington. Companies in this field acquire food from farms, process it, package it, and deliver it to stores. Washington firms process coffee, flour, milk, cheese, and fruit products. Fish and meat canning are also major businesses.

MINING, LOGGING, AND FISHING

Did you know there is gold in Washington's hills? Mines in Chelan and Ferry counties do indeed produce gold. Coal mines operate in Lewis County. Other mines throughout the state produce cement, crushed stone for construction, and sand and gravel.

Products taken from mines and from the land and sea are known as natural resources. Washington is rich in such resources. Along the coast, fishers catch salmon, clams, cod, crabs, and flounder. Oysters are considered

Crab fishers bring in their catch near Westport.

THE LITTLE COMPANY THAT COULD

In 1971, a coffee shop opened in downtown Seattle. It was a small place that sold high-quality coffee beans and equipment. The shop was named Starbucks after a character in the novel *Moby-Dick*. By the early 1980s, the company began selling a variety of coffee drinks. First Seattle and then the nation and the world could not get enough of Starbucks coffee. At one point during the 1990s, the company was opening a new store somewhere in the world every day. Today, there are almost 20,000 Starbucks stores around the world.

Top Products

Agriculture Apples, dairy products, cattle, wheat, hay, potatoes, corn, barley, onions, asparagus, pears, cherries

Manufacturing Airplanes, computers and electronics equipment, food products, ships, medical and communication equipment, wood products, aluminum

Mining Coal, cement, crushed stone, sand and gravel, gold, clay, gypsum, silver

WORD TO KNOW

hydroelectric power *electricity generated by the force of water passing over a dam*

SEE IT HERE!

GRAND COULEE DAM

Construction on the Grand Coulee Dam began in 1933. After nine years of work, the dam was complete. At nearly 1 mile (1.6 km) long, it is the largest concrete structure in North America. It is also the largest producer of hydroelectric power in the United States. Today, visitors to the dam can ride a glass elevator for a marvelous view of the area. They can also view some of the dam's massive generators.

a treat by seafood lovers. The town of Samish, north of Seattle, is a great place to find delicious oysters.

Logging remains a major industry. A pulp and paper firm called the Weyerhaeuser Company began operations in 1900. Weyerhaeuser, which is now headquartered in Federal Way, owns more standing timberland than any other company in the world. Logging is strictly controlled by the state, and every year logging firms plant far more trees than they harvest.

Washington also leads the nation in the production of **hydroelectric power**. The state's greatest single source of hydroelectricity is the Grand Coulee Dam. Other dams in the state also produce electricity and provide water for irrigation. Major dams along the Columbia River include the Bonneville, the Chief Joseph, the John Day, the Dalles, and the Wanapum.

GETTING FROM HERE TO THERE

Washington has some 83,000 miles (134,000 km) of roads and highways. The state's busiest highway—too busy, according to residents—is I-5, which runs north-south through the state from border to border. The major east-west freeway is I-90. Not everyone who commutes to work in Washington drives, takes the bus, or rides a bike.

Logs ready to be shipped from the port of Tacoma

Many people who live on islands in Puget Sound commute by ferry to downtown Seattle.

The Washington coast and Puget Sound have major port facilities where ships from Asia and South America dock. Everett, Seattle, and Tacoma are major ports for oceangoing vessels. The port of Tacoma is specially equipped to load and unload containerships. Such ships carry freight in metal containers the size of railroad cars. Cranes lift the containers on and off the ships with remarkable speed.

Washington's busiest airport is the Seattle-Tacoma International Airport, often called Sea-Tac. The second-largest airport in the state serves Spokane.

BUCKLE UP

According to a 2007 study, 96 percent of Washingtonians use their seat belts while driving. This is the highest percentage of any state.

TRAVEL GUIDE

★

FROM THE THICK FORESTS OF THE OLYMPIC PENINSULA TO THE ARID TERRAIN OF THE COLUMBIA PLATEAU, WASHINGTON IS FILLED WITH BREATHTAKING SCENERY. In between are lively cities and peaceful small towns. In Washington you can ski, hike, and raft. When you get tired, you can go to a rodeo or take a gondola ride. Washington is a big state, and there's a lot to do, so let's get going.

← Follow along with this travel map. We'll begin in the southwest and travel all the way east to Spokane.

SOUTH-WESTERN WASHINGTON

THINGS TO DO: Relax on the beaches, go bird-watching, and learn about Washington's pioneers.

Hoquiam

★ **Grays Harbor National Wildlife Refuge:** Huge numbers of shore-birds stop at this refuge, including sandpipers, dunlins, and plovers. Some of these birds, which are bound for the Arctic, travel more than 15,000 miles (24,000 km) on the round trip from Argentina.

Sandpipers and other birds at Grays Harbor National Wildlife Refuge

You'll find oysters in the Willapa Bay town called Oysterville. You'll also find houses there dating back to the 1800s, when Oysterville was a thriving fishing center.

Washington State International Kite Festival at Long Beach

Long Beach

★ **The beach:** This city boasts just what its name says—the longest sandy beach in the Northwest. Lewis and Clark visited this beach in 1805, and today visitors enjoy volleyball, water sports, the sun's rays, and a kite festival!

Grays River

★ **Grays River Covered Bridge:** This one-lane bridge, built in 1905, is the only covered bridge in Washington still in use by the public.

Vancouver

★ **Fort Vancouver National Historic Site:** The current fort is a replica of the historic fort that was once the center of the vast trading network of the British Hudson's Bay Company in the West.

THE OLYMPIC PENINSULA

THINGS TO DO: Hike through a rain forest, explore an old fort, or get a close look at some beautiful old houses.

Port Townsend

★ **Downtown:** Port Townsend is an old seaport that boasts many ornate **Victorian** buildings.

★ **Fort Flagler State Park:** At this site, you can explore the remains of a U.S. Army fort that once guarded the entrance to Puget Sound. Today, visitors enjoy camping, hiking, biking, and wandering the beach.

Port Gamble

★ **Port Gamble Historic Museum:** Here you can learn what life was like for the pioneers who settled this town in 1853.

WORD TO KNOW

Victorian *a style of architecture that includes the highly decorated houses typical of the reign of Britain's Queen Victoria, who ruled from 1837 to 1901*

SEE IT HERE!

NOT A DISAPPOINTMENT

Near the coastal town of Ilwaco is a point of land called Cape Disappointment. Explorer John Meares gave the spot this name in 1788 because he was disappointed that the cape did not lead to the Columbia River, which he had hoped to find. Few people are disappointed when they visit this scenic land today. The cape is a popular spot for whale watching.

North Head Lighthouse at Cape Disappointment

Chehalis

★ **Lewis County Historical Museum:** This museum displays beautiful baskets made by Native Americans and farm equipment used by Washington pioneers.

SEE IT HERE!

OLYMPIC NATIONAL PARK

Olympic National Park, which spreads over almost 1 million acres (405,000 ha), is a mixture of rain forest, mountains, and beach. In the park's Hoh Rain Forest, which averages more than 12 feet (3.7 m) of rainfall a year, moss-covered trees stand in thick groves. Glaciers top Mount Olympus, while sandy beaches and large boulders alternate on the park's rugged coastline. Few roads penetrate the interior of the park, so the animal habitat remains undisturbed. The park is home to a huge variety of bird and mammal species. Some of the animals that make the park their home are rare, including the Roosevelt elk, and the cougar.

Roosevelt elk

Neah Bay

★ **Makah Cultural and Research Center:** This museum is dedicated to exploring Makah life in the days before Europeans reached the region.

PUGET SOUND AREA

THINGS TO DO: Pet an octopus, ride a ferryboat, or get a bird's-eye view of Seattle.

Seattle

★ **Wing Luke Museum of the Asian Pacific American Experience:** This museum is dedicated to exploring the history and culture of Asian Americans.

★ **Space Needle:** For a thrilling view of Seattle, ride to the top of the Space Needle—its observation platform is more than 500 feet (152 m) high. Built for the 1962 World's Fair, the Space Needle is the city's most prominent landmark.

Downtown Seattle and the Space Needle

Pike Place Market

★ **Pike Place Market:** At this covered market, you can buy fruits and vegetables from farmers, crafts from artisans, and much more. Many people come for the fish, which is just off the boat. Watch out! The fishmongers toss giant salmon to each other.

★ **Seattle Aquarium:** The aquarium displays the sea life of the Pacific Northwest. You can attend daily feedings to get a close look at the aquarium's marine mammal species.

★ **Woodland Park Zoo:** You can see almost 300 species of animals at this world-class zoo—everything from grizzly bears to elephants to kangaroos.

★ **Museum of Flight:** The largest **aviation** museum on the West Coast, the Museum of Flight displays everything from World War I fighter planes to modern jets.

Tacoma

★ **Washington State History Museum:** This interactive museum explores the history of Washington and the people who live there.

WORD TO KNOW

aviation *the design and manufacture of airplanes*

SEE IT HERE!

PUGET SOUND FERRYBOATS

Puget Sound is filled with inlets, peninsulas, and islands. A great way to get around the sound is to ride the Washington State Ferries, which connect the mainland and the islands. Some travel as far north as Canada. The ferries, which serve both commuters and tourists, transport passengers and cars. The sturdy ships are a long-standing symbol of Puget Sound.

★ **Museum of Glass:** This museum, which opened in 2002, houses a world-renowned collection of glass-works and art.

★ **Point Defiance Park:** This park sprawls over 700 acres (283 ha). It includes a zoo, an aquarium, beaches, gardens, trails, and an old-growth forest.

Olympia

★ **Washington State Capitol:** In the city center stands the 28-story capitol, which is surrounded by gardens.

THE CASCADES

THINGS TO DO: Peer into a volcano, see a glacier, or kayak through a pristine wilderness.

Camping in Mount Rainier National Park

Ashford

★ **Mount Rainier National Park:** The snowcapped peak of Mount Rainier rises 14,410 feet (4,392 m) and dominates southwestern Washington. Around two million visitors a year come to this park to hike, mountain climb, and ski.

Emmons Glacier, in Mount Rainier National Park, is the largest glacier in the United States outside of Alaska.

Visitors' reflections in the Seaform Pavilion by Dale Chihuly at Tacoma's Museum of Glass

SEE IT HERE!

MOUNT ST. HELENS

On May 18, 1980, Mount St. Helens was a snowcapped mountain with a perfectly round top. Then, in the blink of an eye, it changed. When the mountain erupted, it lost 1,312 feet (400 m) off its top. Debris and ash destroyed forests for miles around. Visitors can take a helicopter tour of the once-devastated region where forests are now growing again.

Tourists at Mount St. Helens

Sedro-Woolley

★ **North Cascades National Park:** This mountain landscape includes more than 300 glaciers. The park supports a wide variety of wildlife, including bald eagles, wolves, beavers, and grizzly bears. Visitors to the park enjoy backpacking, kayaking, and canoeing.

CENTRAL WASHINGTON

THINGS TO DO: Feast on German food, ride a trolley car, or raft down a roaring river.

Ellensburg

★ **Ellensburg Rodeo:** The Ellensburg Rodeo attracts cowboys and cowgirls from all over the nation. It has been held since 1923 and is considered one of the nation's best.

Yakima

★ **Yakima Electric Railway Museum:** An extensive collection of vintage trolley cars is on display.
★ **Yakima River Canyon:** Some visitors come here to enjoy a peaceful bicycle ride or see the abundant wildlife, which includes bald eagles and bighorn sheep. Others head to the Tieton River for some wild white-water rafting.

A train running through Yakima River Canyon

Toppenish

★ **Yakama Nation Museum and Cultural Center:** Learn about the Yakama people through exhibits on their dwellings, jewelry, clothing, and much more.

Leavenworth

★ **Downtown:** In the early 1960s, the former logging town of Leavenworth was dying economically. So Leavenworth's leaders redesigned the town to make it look like a German village. It now boasts German-style houses, German-style restaurants, and German-themed festivals.

A horse-drawn carriage in Leavenworth

EASTERN WASHINGTON

THINGS TO DO: Swim in a lake whose waters feel soapy, see how Washington pioneers lived, or tour Washington's second-largest city.

Soap Lake

★ **Soap Lake:** This lake was named Soap Lake because the pioneers thought that swimming in it left their skin with a soapy feeling. In fact, Soap Lake has an unusual mineral content, and Native Americans once used its waters as medicine.

Coulee Dam

★ **Lake Roosevelt National Recreation Area:** Created by the Grand Coulee Dam, this lake is 130 miles (209 km) long. Vacationers rent houseboats to enjoy the lake at a leisurely pace.

Pasco

★ **Sacajawea State Park:** This park, which is located where the Snake River flows into the Columbia, is named after the Shoshone woman who served as a guide for Lewis and Clark. The expedition camped in the area in 1805.

Walla Walla

★ **Fort Walla Walla Museum:** Here you can learn how people lived in pioneer settlements. Costumed guides demonstrate traditional skills and explain what life was like in the area in the second half of the 19th century.

Visitors at Fort Walla Walla

FAQ

Q WHAT DOES THE NAME WALLA WALLA MEAN?

A It comes from a Native American word that means running waters, referring to the many streams in the area.

★ **Riverfront Park:** In the heart of Spokane is Riverfront Park, a 100-acre (40 ha) playground for the city. Visitors can thrill to a "SkyRide" over Spokane Falls or ride on a historic carousel built in 1909, which features hand-carved wooden horses.

Spokane

★ **Northwest Museum of Arts & Culture:** This museum includes more than 68,000 objects, with an emphasis on regional culture. Exhibits include everything from Native American beadwork to pioneer quilts to contemporary paintings.

The clock tower at Riverfront Park

SCIENCE, TECHNOLOGY, ENGINEERING, & MATH PROJECTS

120

Make weather maps, graph population statistics, and research endangered species that live in the state.

PRIMARY VS. SECONDARY SOURCES

121

So what are primary and secondary sources? And what's the diff? This section explains all that and where you can find them.

BIOGRAPHICAL DICTIONARY

133

This at-a-glance guide highlights some of the state's most important and influential people. Visit this section and read about their contributions to the state, the country, and the world.

RESOURCES

Books and much more. Take a look at these additional sources for information about the state.

138

WRITING PROJECTS

Create an Election Brochure or Web Site!

Run for office! Throughout this book, you've read about some of the issues that concern Washington today. As a candidate for governor of Washington, create a campaign brochure or Web site.

★ Explain how you meet the qualifications to be governor of Washington.

★ Talk about the three or four major issues you'll focus on if you're elected.

★ Remember, you'll be responsible for Washington's budget. How would you spend the taxpayers' money?

SEE: Chapter Seven, pages 87–89.

Create an interview script with a famous person from Washington!

★ Research various Washingtonians, such as Sealth, May Hutton, Janet McCloud, Jimi Hendrix, Sherman Alexie, Gary Locke, or Bill Gates.

★ Based on your research, pick one person you would most like to talk with.

★ Write a script of the interview. What questions would you ask? How would this person answer? Create a question-and-answer format. You may want to supplement this writing project with a voice-recording dramatization of the interview.

SEE: Chapters Four, Five, Six, Seven, Eight, pages 46, 59, 68, 80, 81, 89, and 101, and the Biographical Dictionary, pages 133–137.

Write a Memoir, Journal Entry, or Editorial for Your School Newspaper!

Picture Yourself . . .

★ Giving a potlatch. Why did your family decide to host a potlatch? How do they prepare for it? What happens at the feast?
  SEE: Chapter Two, page 29.

★ As a Japanese American living in Seattle at the beginning of World War II. Write a series of journal entries about your experiences. Describe your feelings when you hear about the order forcing people of Japanese heritage into internment camps. Explain how your family prepares for the move. Describe the sights, sounds, and smells of living in the camp. What do you and the other kids do for fun? What do you miss from home?
  SEE: Chapter Five, pages 62–64.

ART PROJECTS

Create a PowerPoint Presentation or Visitors' Guide

Welcome to Washington!

Washington's a great place to visit and to live! From its natural beauty to its historical sites, there's plenty to see and do. In your PowerPoint presentation or brochure, highlight 10 to 15 of Washington's fascinating landmarks. Be sure to include:

★ a map of the state showing where these sites are located

★ photos, illustrations, Web links, natural history facts, geographic stats, climate and weather, plants and wildlife, and recent discoveries

SEE: Chapter Nine, pages 106–115, and Fast Facts, pages 126–127.

Illustrate the Lyrics to the Washington State Song

("Washington, My Home!")

Use markers, paints, photos, collages, colored pencils, or computer graphics to illustrate the lyrics to "Washington, My Home!" Turn your illustrations into a picture book, or scan them into PowerPoint and add music.

SEE: The lyrics to "Washington, My Home!" on page 128.

Research Washington's State Quarter

From 1999 to 2008, the U.S. Mint introduced new quarters commemorating each of the 50 states in the order that they were admitted to the Union. Each state's quarter features a unique design on its reverse, or back.

★ Research the significance of the image. Who designed the quarter? Who chose the final design?

★ Design your own Washington quarter. What images would you choose for the reverse?

★ Make a poster showing the Washington quarter and label each image.

GO TO: www.factsfornow.scholastic.com. Enter the keyword **Washington** and look for the link to the Washington quarter.

SCIENCE, TECHNOLOGY, ENGINEERING, & MATH PROJECTS

Graph Population Statistics!

★ Compare population statistics (such as ethnic background, birth, death, and literacy rates) in Washington counties or major cities.

★ In your graph or chart, look at population density and write sentences describing what the population statistics show; graph one set of population statistics and write a paragraph explaining what the graphs reveal.

SEE: Chapter Six, pages 72–75.

Create a Weather Map of Washington!

Use your knowledge of Washington's geography to research and identify conditions that result in specific weather events, including snow and persistent rainfall. What is it about the geography of Washington that makes it vulnerable to this wet weather? Create a weather map or poster that shows the weather patterns over the state, or display wet and dry years between 1895 and the present. Include a caption explaining the technology used to measure weather phenomena and provide data.

SEE: Chapter One, pages 18–19.

Gray wolf

Track Endangered Species

Using your knowledge of Washington's wildlife, research which animals and plants are endangered or threatened.

★ Find out what the state is doing to protect these species.

★ Chart known populations of the animals and plants, and report on changes in certain geographic areas.

SEE: Chapter One, page 22.

PRIMARY VS. SECONDARY SOURCES

What's the Diff?

Your teacher may require at least one or two primary sources and one or two secondary sources for your assignment. So, what's the difference between the two?

★ **Primary sources are original.** You are reading the actual words of someone's diary, journal, letter, autobiography, or interview. Primary sources can also be photographs, maps, prints, cartoons, news/film footage, posters, first-person newspaper articles, drawings, musical scores, and recordings. By the way, when you conduct a survey, interview someone, shoot a video, or take photographs to include in a project, you are creating primary sources!

★ **Secondary sources are what you find in encyclopedias, textbooks, articles, biographies, and almanacs.** These are written by a person or group of people who tell about something that happened to someone else. Secondary sources also recount what another person said or did. This book is an example of a secondary source.

Now that you know what primary sources are—where can you find them?

★ **Your school or local library:** Check the library catalog for collections of original writings, government documents, musical scores, and so on. Some of this material may be stored on microfilm.

★ **Historical societies:** These organizations keep historical documents, photographs, and other materials. Staff members can help you find what you are looking for. History museums are also great places to see primary sources firsthand.

★ **The Internet:** There are lots of sites that have primary sources you can download and use in a project or assignment.

TIMELINE

U.S. Events		Washington Events
	10,000 BCE	

c. 10,000 BCE
The first people arrive in what is now Washington.

8000 BCE

c. 8000 BCE
Early Native people establish a settlement near Moses Lake.

1 CE

c. 1 CE
Cultures of peoples east and west of the Cascades diverge.

Artifacts from Moses Lake

1600

1607
The first permanent English settlement in North America is established at Jamestown.

1620
Pilgrims found Plymouth Colony, the second permanent English settlement.

1700

Early 1700s
People in the Pacific Northwest acquire horses.

Early 1700s
Traders bring metal tools to the region.

1775
Spanish explorer Bruno de Heceta leads the first group of Europeans to set foot in what is now Washington.

1776
Thirteen American colonies declare their independence from Great Britain.

1787
The U.S. Constitution is written.

1792
George Vancouver names Mount Rainier, Mount Baker, and Puget Sound; Robert Gray claims the Washington area for the United States.

Robert Gray

U.S. Events | 1800 | Washington Events

1803

The Louisiana Purchase almost doubles the size of the United States.

1805

Lewis and Clark reach the Pacific Ocean at the mouth of the Columbia River.

1830

The Indian Removal Act forces eastern Native American groups to relocate west of the Mississippi River.

1836

Marcus and Narcissa Whitman establish a mission church near Walla Walla.

1846–48

The United States fights a war with Mexico over western territories in the Mexican War.

1847

Native Americans try to force whites off their land during the Cayuse War.

1852

Seattle is founded.

1853

Washington Territory is established.

Chief Joseph

1859

Great Britain and the United States nearly go to war over a pig.

1861–65

The American Civil War is fought between the Northern Union and the Southern Confederacy; it ends with the surrender of the Confederate army, led by General Robert E. Lee.

1877

Chief Joseph leads the Nez Perce on a long retreat.

1883

The Northern Pacific Railway is completed, connecting Tacoma with Chicago.

1886

Apache leader Geronimo surrenders to the U.S. Army, ending the last major Native American rebellion against the expansion of the United States into the West.

1898

The United States gains control of Puerto Rico, the Philippines, and Guam after defeating Spain in the Spanish-American War.

1889

Washington becomes the 42nd state.

1897

Seattle booms after gold is discovered in Alaska.

124

U.S. Events `1900` **Washington Events**

1910
Washington passes a law allowing women to vote in state elections.

1917–18
The United States engages in World War I.

1929
The stock market crashes, plunging the United States more deeply into the Great Depression.

1933
Work begins on Bonneville Dam on the Columbia River.

1941–45
The United States engages in World War II.

1942
The Grand Coulee Dam, the largest concrete dam in North America, is completed.

1942–45
Japanese Americans are forced into internment camps during World War II.

1950–53
The United States engages in the Korean War.

1962
The Seattle World's Fair opens.

1964–73
The United States engages in the Vietnam War.

1974
A court decision guarantees Native Americans the right to fish in traditional areas; Spokane holds a world's fair.

1980
Mount St. Helens erupts.

1991
The United States and other nations engage in the brief Persian Gulf War against Iraq.

1996
Gary Locke is elected the first Chinese American governor of any state.

`2000`

2001
Terrorists hijack four U.S. aircraft and crash them into the World Trade Center in New York City, the Pentagon in Arlington, Virginia, and a Pennsylvania field, killing thousands.

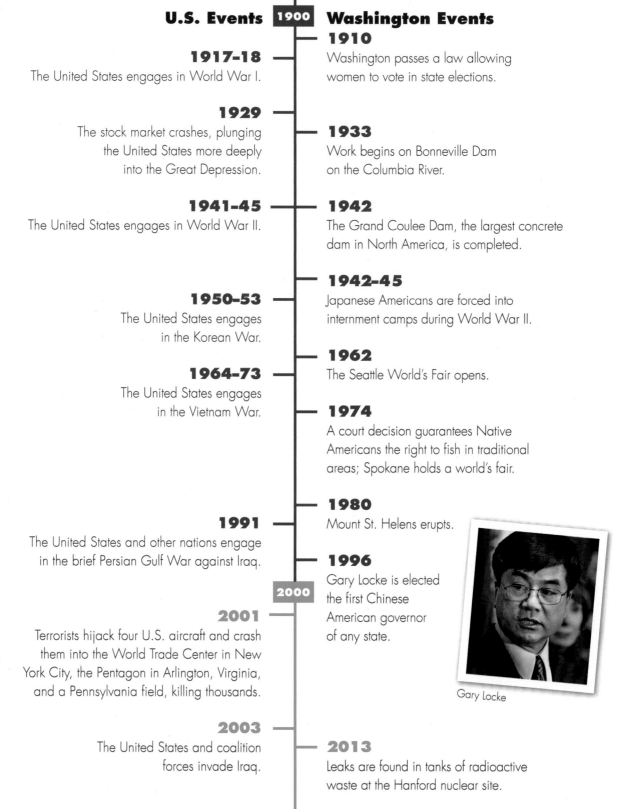

Gary Locke

2003
The United States and coalition forces invade Iraq.

2013
Leaks are found in tanks of radioactive waste at the Hanford nuclear site.

GLOSSARY

★ ★ ★

archaeologists people who study the remains of past human societies

arid dry

attorney general chief legal adviser and law officer

auditor someone who checks financial accounts

aviation the design and manufacture of airplanes

discrimination unequal treatment based on race, gender, religion, or other factors

ecology the study of relationships between living things and their environment

erosion the wearing away of rock or soil by wind, water, or other factors

general strike an organized refusal to work by all workers in a city or region

geologists scientists who study the history of Earth

hydroelectric power electricity generated by the force of water passing over a dam

immunities natural protections against diseases

impelled forced somebody to do something

incorporated recognized as a self-governing organization

latitude the position of a place, measured in degrees north or south of the equator

missionaries people who try to convert others to a religion

plateau an elevated part of the earth with steep slopes

prejudice an unreasonable hatred or fear of others based on race, religion, ethnic group, gender, or other factors

rescinds declares null and void

runoff water from rain or snow that flows over the ground and into streams

solidarity unity that is based on shared interests or goals

strait a narrow passageway of water that connects larger bodies of water

suffrage the right to vote

Victorian a style of architecture that includes the highly decorated houses typical of the reign of Britain's Queen Victoria, who ruled from 1837 to 1901

FAST FACTS

★ ★ ★

State Symbols

Statehood date	November 11, 1889, 42nd state
Origin of state name	Named for George Washington, the first U.S. president
State capital	Olympia
State nickname	Evergreen State
State motto	*Alki* ("Bye and Bye")
State bird	Willow goldfinch
State flower	Coast rhododendron
State fish	Steelhead trout
State gem	Petrified wood
State song	"Washington, My Home!" (See lyrics on page 128)
State tree	Western hemlock
State dance	Square dance

State seal

Geography

Total area; rank	71,298 square miles (184,661 sq km); 18th
Land area; rank	66,449 square miles (172,102 sq km); 20th
Water area; rank	4,849 square miles (12,559 sq km); 11th
Inland water; rank	1,646 square miles (4,263 sq km); 14th
Coastal water; rank	2,537 square miles (6,571 sq km); 2nd
Territorial water; rank	666 square miles (1,725 sq km); 12th
Geographic center	Chelan County, 10 miles (16 km) west-southwest of Wenatchee
Latitude	45°32' N to 49° N
Longitude	116°57' W to 124°48' W
Highest point	Mount Rainier, 14,410 feet (4,392 m), located in Pierce County
Lowest point	Sea level along the Pacific Ocean
Largest city	Seattle
Number of counties	39
Longest river	Columbia River

Population

Population; rank (2010 census)	6,724,540; 13th
Density (2010 census)	101 persons per square mile (39 per sq km)
Population distribution (2010 census)	84% urban, 16% rural
Ethnic distribution (2010 census)	White persons: 72.5%
	Persons of Hispanic or Latino origin: 11.2%
	Asian persons: 7.1%
	Persons reporting two or more races: 3.7%
	Black persons: 3.4%
	American Indian and Alaska Native persons: 1.3%
	Native Hawaiian and other Pacific Islanders: 0.6%
	Persons of some other race: 0.2%

Weather

Record high temperature	118°F (48°C) at Wahluke on July 24, 1928, and at Ice Harbor Dam on August 5, 1961
Record low temperature	−48°F (−44°C) at Mazama and Winthrop on December 30, 1968
Average July temperature, Seattle	67°F (19°C)
Average January temperature, Seattle	42°F (6°C)
Average yearly precipitation, Seattle	40 inches (102 cm)

State flag

STATE SONG

★ ★ ★

"Washington, My Home!"

This was chosen as the state song in 1959. It was written by Helen Davis and arranged by Stuart Churchill.

This is my country; God gave it to me;
I will protect it, ever keep it free.
Small towns and cities rest here in the sun,
Filled with our laughter, "Thy will be done."

Washington my home;
Where ever I may roam;
This is my land, my native land,
Washington, my home.
Our verdant forest green,
Caressed by silvery stream;
From mountain peak to fields of wheat.
Washington, my home.

There's peace you feel and understand
In this, our own beloved land.
We greet the day with head held high,
And forward ever is our cry.
We'll happy ever be
As people always free.
For you and me a destiny;
Washington, my home.

NATURAL AREAS AND HISTORIC SITES

★ ★ ★

National Park

Mount Rainier National Park features its namesake, an active volcano encased in snow and ice, where many people go to enjoy snowshoeing, cross-country skiing, and hiking.

North Cascades National Park features rugged peaks, deep valleys, stunning waterfalls, and glaciers inhabited by diverse plants and animals.

Olympic National Park protects dense rain forests, soaring mountains, and isolated beaches.

National Historical Parks

Klondike Gold Rush-Seattle Unit National Historical Park focuses on Seattle's role in the Alaskan gold rush of 1897–1898.

Nez Perce National Historical Park recalls the stories and history of the Nez Perce people.

San Juan Island National Historical Park tells the story of the Pig War, when Great Britain and the United States vied for the islands.

National Historic Sites

Fort Vancouver National Historic Site includes a replica of the Hudson's Bay Company trading post that was the center of much activity in the Pacific Northwest in the early to mid-1800s.

The *Whitman Mission National Historic Site* commemorates the role Narcissa and Marcus Whitman played in establishing the Oregon Trail.

National Historical Reserve

Ebey's Landing National Historical Reserve preserves a rural settlement that has existed since the 19th century on Whidbey Island in Puget Sound. The landscape includes prairies, sea bluffs, woodlands, and a cove.

National Historic Trail

The *Lewis & Clark National Historic Trail*, which follows the route taken by the Lewis and Clark expedition, passes through Washington. Much of the trail runs along the Missouri and Columbia rivers.

National Recreation Areas

Washington's three national recreation areas are *Lake Chelan National Recreation Area*, *Lake Roosevelt National Recreation Area*, and *Ross Lake National Recreation Area*.

State Parks and Forests

Washington's state park system features 140 state parks and recreation areas, including *Lewis and Clark State Park*, *Ocean City State Park*, and *Rainbow Falls State Park*.

SPORTS TEAMS

★ ★ ★

NCAA Teams (Division I)

Eastern Washington University *Eagles*
Gonzaga University *Bulldogs*
Seattle University *Redhawks*
University of Washington *Huskies*
Washington State University *Cougars*

PROFESSIONAL SPORTS TEAMS

★ ★ ★

Major League Baseball

Seattle *Mariners*

National Football League

Seattle *Seahawks*

Women's National Basketball Association

Seattle *Storm*

Major League Soccer

Seattle *Sounders FC*

CULTURAL INSTITUTIONS

★   ★   ★

Libraries

Washington State Library (Olympia) is the state's oldest library and contains excellent collections on Washington history.

The *Seattle Public Library* contains fine collections on the Pacific Northwest.

The *University of Washington Library* (Seattle) contains a major collection on East Asia, Pacific Northwest history, and the fishing industry.

Museums

The *Burke Museum of Natural History and Culture* (Seattle) features exhibits on natural history and the Native Americans of Washington.

The *Seattle Art Museum* has strong collections of African and Northwest Native American art.

The *Washington State History Museum* (Tacoma) has exhibits on life in the state.

The *Seattle Asian Art Museum* emphasizes Chinese and Japanese art but also displays work from other parts of Asia.

The *Northwest Museum of Arts & Culture* (Spokane) has exhibits on Native American culture and regional history.

Performing Arts

The *Seattle Symphony*, founded in 1903, performs groundbreaking modern works and classical compositions at Benaroya Hall in downtown Seattle.

The *Tacoma Opera* offers traditional and nontraditional productions performed by nationally and regionally known artists.

Universities and Colleges

In 2011, Washington had 16 public and 33 private institutions of higher learning.

ANNUAL EVENTS

January–March
Bavarian Ice Fest in Leavenworth (January)

Skagit Eagle Festival (January)

Seattle Boat Show in Seattle (January–February)

International Snowshoe Softball Tournament in Winthrop (February)

Northwest Bach Festival in Spokane (February–March)

April–June
Daffodil Festival in Pierce County (April)

Cherry Blossom and Japanese Cultural Festival in Seattle (April)

Washington State Apple Blossom Festival in Wenatchee (April–May)

Lilac Bloomsday Run in Spokane (May)

Annual Rhododendron Festival in Port Townsend (late May)

Seafair in Seattle (June–August)

July–September
Toppenish Rodeo in Toppenish (July)

Bellevue Festival of the Arts in Bellevue (July)

King County Fair in Enumclaw (July)

Port Townshend Acoustic Blues Workshop in Port Townsend (July–August)

Omak Stampede and World Famous Suicide Race (August)

International Kite Festival in Long Beach (August)

Evergreen State Fair in Monroe (August–September)

Ellensburg Rodeo (September)

Washington State Fair in Puyallup (September)

Washington State Autumn Leaf Festival in Leavenworth (September)

October–December
OysterFest in Shelton (October)

Oktoberfest in Leavenworth (October)

Nathan Adrian (1988–), a native of Bremerton, is a freestyle swimmer who has won three Olympic gold medals. He began swimming competitively at the age of five and went on to win five National Collegiate Athletic Association (NCAA) championships at the University of California–Berkeley.

Sherman Alexie See page 81.

Paul Allen (1953–) cofounded Microsoft with Bill Gates in 1975. Allen left the company in the 1980s and promotes many different projects in aeronautics, brain science, and other fields. One of the world's richest people, he owns the Seattle Seahawks football team, the Portland Trail Blazers basketball team, and part of the Seattle Sounders FC soccer team. He was born in Seattle.

Earl Averill (1902–1983), a Hall of Fame baseball player, was born in Snohomish. He played for several teams and retired with a .318 lifetime batting average.

William Boeing (1881–1956) founded the Boeing Company in Seattle in 1916. Today, it is the largest aircraft manufacturer in the world.

J Harlen Bretz (1882–1981) was a geologist who uncovered the secrets of Washington's Channeled Scablands.

Linda Brown Buck (1947–), a native of Seattle and a graduate of the University of Washington, won the Nobel Prize in Physiology or Medicine in 2004 for her discoveries relating to humans' sense of smell.

Carlos Bulosan (1911?–1956) was a novelist who moved from the Philippines to Washington at age 17. He worked harvesting crops, in hotels, and in canneries, and became active in the union movement. His novel *America Is in the Heart* recounts some of his experiences.

Carlos Bulosan

George Washington Bush See page 43.

Raymond Carver (1938–1988) was a short-story writer and poet who grew up in Yakima. His acclaimed stories often concern everyday people living troubled lives. His works include the story collections *Will You Please Be Quiet, Please?* and *Where I'm Calling From*.

Carol Channing (1921–) is a singer and actress best known for her work in the musical *Hello, Dolly!* She was born in Seattle.

Ray Charles (1930–2004), who was born in Georgia and went blind as a child, lived in Seattle as a young man. He combined blues, gospel, and jazz, helping create a new style of music called soul. His classic songs include "Hit the Road Jack," "What'd I Say," and "Georgia on My Mind."

Dale Chihuly (1941–) is an artist who designs blown-glass creations. He was born in Tacoma.

Ray Charles

Chuck Close (1940–) is a painter and photographer who makes large-scale portraits. He was born in Monroe.

Kurt Cobain See page 80.

Judy Collins (1939–) is a folksinger and songwriter who had hit songs such as "Send in the Clowns" and "Amazing Grace." She was born in Seattle.

Judy Collins

Fred Couples (1959–) is a professional golfer who is known as "Boom Boom" because of his long drives. He was born in Seattle.

Bing Crosby (1903–1977) is one of the most popular singers of his time. He had 41 number-one hit singles, including "White Christmas," the best-selling single of all time. He also starred in dozens of movies. He was born in Tacoma.

Merce Cunningham (1919–2009) was a modern dancer and choreographer who began his career with Martha Graham's dance company. In 1953, he formed the Merce Cunningham Dance Company. He was born in Centralia.

Arthur A. Denny (1822–1899) was born in Indiana and led the Denny Party west to the Puget Sound area in 1851. There he became one of the founders of Seattle.

Gail Devers (1966–) is a three-time Olympic gold medal winner in track and field. Born in Seattle, she is a member of both the National Track and Field Hall of Fame and the U.S. Olympic Hall of Fame.

John Elway (1960–), born in Port Angeles, was one of the greatest quarterbacks in NFL history. He led the Denver Broncos to two Super Bowl victories.

Frederick Schiller Faust (1892–1944) was a popular writer who wrote under the name Max Brand. He thrilled millions of readers with his Western novels such as *Destry Rides Again*. He was born in Seattle.

Elisha P. Ferry See page 53.

Tom Foley See page 91.

Bill Gates See page 101.

Christine Gregoire (1947–) was elected governor of Washington in 2004 in one of the closest elections in history. Prior to becoming governor, she served as the state attorney general. She was born in Auburn.

Jimi Hendrix (1942–1970), who was born in Seattle, is considered one of the greatest guitar players in the history of rock music. He was influenced by blues and jazz and often made music using feedback.

Frank Herbert (1920–1986) was a science-fiction writer best known for the novel *Dune*. He was born in Tacoma.

May Hutton See page 59.

Henry Jackson (1912–1983) was a powerful politician who served as a U.S. senator from Washington for 30 years. He was born in Everett.

Jimi Hendrix

Chuck Jones (1912–2002) was a wildly inventive animator and director of cartoons who was born in Spokane. He created classic characters such as Road Runner, Wile E. Coyote, and Pepé Le Pew.

Chuck Jones

Kamiakin (1800?–1877) was a Yakama leader who led his nation in the 1855 war with white settlers.

Phyllis Gutiérrez Kenney See page 90.

Henry "Hank" Ketcham (1920–2001), a native of Seattle, was a cartoonist best known for creating the comic strip *Dennis the Menace*, which he wrote and drew from 1951 to 1994. The strip continues today, drawn and written by other creators.

Bertha Knight Landes (1868–1943) was a political leader who was elected mayor of Seattle in 1926. She was the first woman to be elected mayor of a large American city.

Steve Largent (1954–) is a Hall of Fame football player who played wide receiver for the Seattle Seahawks for 13 years. He was legendary for almost never dropping a pass. After retiring from football, he represented Oklahoma in the U.S. Congress.

Gary Larson (1950–) is an artist who created *The Far Side*, a comic strip in which he often compared the behavior of animals and humans. He was born in Tacoma.

Gary Larson

Jacob Lawrence See page 79.

Tim Lincecum (1984–) is a two-time winner of baseball's National League Cy Young Award. He helped lead his team, the San Francisco Giants, to World Series championships in 2010 and 2012. He was born in Bellevue.

Mary Livingstone (1905–1983) was an actor and comedian who was married to comedy great Jack Benny and frequently appeared on his radio show. She was born in Seattle.

Gary Locke See page 89.

Betty MacDonald (1908–1958) was an author who wrote several humorous books about her own life. In *The Egg and I*, she wrote of her failed attempt to be a chicken farmer on the Olympic Peninsula. She also wrote a series of children's books about Mrs. Piggle-Wiggle. She grew up in Seattle.

Macklemore (1983–) is a Seattle-born rapper whose birth name is Ben Haggerty. His singles "Thrift Shop" and "Can't Hold Us" both reached number one on the *Billboard* Hot 100 chart in 2013. In 2014, he won four Grammy Awards, including Best New Artist and Best Rap Album.

Betty MacDonald

Phil Mahre

Phil Mahre (1957–) is an Olympic skier who won a gold medal in 1984 in the slalom event. His twin brother, Steve, won the silver in the same event. The Mahre brothers were born in Yakima.

David "Doc" Maynard (1808–1873), a native of Vermont, was one of the founders of the city of Seattle as well as its first doctor. He was a friend of the Squamish leader Sealth and worked to have Seattle named after the famous Native American leader.

Mary McCarthy (1912–1989) was an author who wrote prizewinning novels and short stories, including *The Company She Keeps* and *The Group*. She was born in Seattle.

Janet McCloud See page 68.

Joel McHale (1971–) is an actor best known for hosting the television program *The Soup* and for his role as Jeff Winger in the comedy series *Community*. He grew up in Seattle.

Mark Morris (1956–) is a choreographer who heads the Mark Morris Dance Group. His work is renowned for its humor and inventiveness. He grew up in Seattle.

Robert Motherwell (1915–1991) was an artist who made abstract paintings, often using stark black paint. He was born in Aberdeen.

Patty Murray (1950–) is the first woman to serve as a U.S. senator from Washington. A Democrat who was born in Bothell, she began serving in the Senate in 1993.

Edward R. Murrow (1908–1965), who grew up in Blanchard, was a radio and TV reporter during and after World War II. He was renowned for his honesty and integrity.

Apolo Anton Ohno (1982–) is a champion short-track speed skater. He won gold medals at both the 2002 and the 2006 Olympics. He was born in Federal Way.

Robert Osborne (1932–) is a film historian and host for Turner Classic Movies, a cable television channel that broadcasts famous films of the past. Born in Colfax, he was awarded a star on the Hollywood Walk of Fame in 2006.

Randall Beth Platt (1948–) writes books for young people, such as *The Likes of Me* and *The Cornerstone*. She was born in Seattle.

Dixy Lee Ray (1914–1994) was a professor of biology at the University of Washington before being elected the state's first female governor in 1976. She was born in Tacoma.

Dixy Lee Ray

Ann Reinking (1949–) is an actress and dancer born in Seattle. She is best known for her performances on Broadway in *Dancin'*, *A Chorus Line*, and *Sweet Charity*, and the films *Annie* and *Micki & Maude*.

Hilary Swank

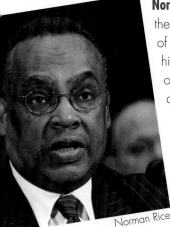

Norman Rice

Norman Rice (1943–) became the first African American mayor of Seattle in 1990. During his two terms in office, he oversaw the revitalization of downtown Seattle.

Sacagawea See page 37.

Ron Santo (1940–2010), who was born in Seattle, overcame childhood diabetes to become a star third baseman with the Chicago Cubs.

Dick Scobee (1939–1986), born in Cle Elum, was the commander of the space shuttle *Challenger*, which exploded in midair seconds after takeoff. He and the six other astronauts on board were killed in the accident.

Sealth See page 46.

Tom Sneva (1948–) is a race-car driver who was named to the Motorsports Hall of Fame of America in 2005. In 1977, he was the first driver to break the 200-mile-per-hour (322 kph) mark at the Indianapolis time trials.

Gary Snyder (1930–), who has won such major poetry awards as the Ruth Lilly Poetry Prize and the Bollingen Prize, spent much of his childhood in the Puget Sound area. His poetry collections include *Turtle Island* and *The Real Work*.

Isaac Stevens (1818–1862) was the first governor of Washington Territory and a U.S. congressman. During the Civil War, he served in the Union army and was killed at the Battle of Chantilly in Virginia.

Hilary Swank (1974–) is a film actor who has appeared in films such as *Million Dollar Baby* and *P.S. I Love You*. She has won the Academy Award for Best Actress twice. She grew up in Bellingham.

George Vancouver (1757–1798) was a British explorer and sea captain. He named many Washington landmarks, including Puget Sound and Mount Rainier.

Adam West (1928–) is an actor who played Batman in a popular 1960s TV series. He was born in Walla Walla.

Audrey May Wurdemann (1911–1960) was a poet who was born in Seattle. She won the Pulitzer Prize for Poetry in 1935 for *Bright Ambush*.

Minoru Yamasaki (1912–1986) was an architect who designed New York City's World Trade Center, which was destroyed in the September 11, 2001, terrorist attacks. He was born in Seattle.

Takuji Yamashita See page 64.

RESOURCES

★ ★ ★   ★ ★

BOOKS

Nonfiction

Brown, Cynthia L. *Geology of the Pacific Northwest: Investigate How the Earth Was Formed with 15 Projects*. White River Junction, Vt.: Nomad Press, 2011.

Demuth, Patricia. *Who Is Bill Gates?* New York: Grosset & Dunlap, 2013.

Domnauer, Teresa. *The Lewis & Clark Expedition*. New York: Children's Press, 2013.

Friedman, Mel. *The Oregon Trail*. New York: Children's Press, 2013.

Marsico, Katie. *Puget Sound*. Ann Arbor, Mich.: Cherry Lake Publishers, 2013.

Sanford, William R., and Carl R. Green. *Sacagawea: Courageous American Indian Guide*. Berkeley Heights, N.J.: Enslow Publishers, 2013.

Strudwick, Leslie. *Washington: The Evergreen State*. New York: AV2 by Weigl, 2012.

Fiction

Alexie, Sherman. *The Absolutely True Diary of a Part-Time Indian*. New York: Little Brown, 2007.

Caletti, Deb. *The Fortunes of Indigo Skye*. New York: Simon and Schuster Books for Young Readers, 2008.

Patneaude, David. *Thin Wood Walls*. Boston: Houghton Mifflin, 2004.

Platt, Randall Beth. *The Likes of Me*. New York: Delacorte Press, 2000.

Sullivan, Jacqueline Levering. *Annie's War*. Grand Rapids, Mich.: Eerdmans Books for Young Readers, 2007.

Visit this Scholastic Web site for more information on Washington:
www.factsfornow.scholastic.com
Enter the keyword **Washington**

INDEX

★ ★ ★

AUTHOR'S TIPS AND SOURCE NOTES

★ ★ ★

I consulted many books in my research for this project. *Washington's History* by Harry Ritter and *Compass American Guides: Washington* by John Doerper were particularly helpful. *Washington: A Guide to the Evergreen State* is an old book—it was written in 1941—but is still a great read. Of course, I also did extensive research on the Internet. Some of what you see online is untrustworthy, but you can usually rely on government, library, museum, and university Web sites to provide accurate information.